COMMUNICATING WITH THE ADOPTED CHILD

COMMUNICATING WITH THE ADOPTED CHILD

by Miriam Komar, D.S.W.

WALKER AND COMPANY
New York

The conversations reproduced in the text are real, but names and other
identifying information has been changed to protect the confidentiality of all
who participated in this research.

First published in the United States of America in 1991
by Walker Publishing Company, Inc.
Published simultaneously in Canada by Thomas Allen & Son
Canada, Limited, Markham, Ontario

Library of Congress Cataloging-in-Publication Data

Komar, Miriam.
Communicating with the adopted child / by Miriam Komar.
Includes bibliographical references and index.
ISBN 0-8027-1124-3
1. Children, Adopted—United States—Case studies.
I. Title.
HV875.55.K65   1990
362.7'34—dc20   90-38340

Printed in the United States of America

2   4   6   8   10   9   7   5   3   1

For all those whose open-hearted willingness
to share their experiences and insights
made this book possible
And
For Hegeman, whose support
and encouragement meant so much

Contents

Introduction

There are one million adopted children in the United States eighteen years and under. Their loving parents are concerned with the best way to help these children with their questions about themselves. All parents, of course, have a concern over communicating with their children, but the adoptive situation demands an exquisite attention and a particular sensitivity to the needs of the adopted child for knowledge and comfort. Most families are twice linked: once through their physical bond and a second time through the strength of communication. Adoptive families depend entirely on the link of two-way touch and talk.

Sadly, studies indicate that adoptees often do not feel comfortable talking about their ongoing questions and concerns with their adoptive parents. My goal in writing this book is to help parents recognize a powerful tool they already have for solving this problem: ordinary family conversations. When parents know how to talk about what the adoptive experience means to a child, their hearts will lead them to express their love and support in the words that will be most effective.

What you'll find in these pages is a guide to the *how* and *what* of talking about adoptive issues: not just once, but over and over, throughout all stages of childhood development. The book also provides information about the *how* of family communication—the power of speech itself to convey emotional support and encourage intellectual understanding. All the people you'll meet here are real: every example in the book is based on actual verbatim conversations in families who have generously agreed to share their successes and failures. You'll hear ordinary parents being confronted by their adoptive children in everyday family situations, and you'll see why some responses are useful and others are not. What you won't find are "recipes" and rote answers. In real life, there is no one right answer to a question, for the effectiveness of any communication is linked to the specific people involved. The major priority is to comprehend the underlying meaning of a child's words and actions. Based on this knowledge, parents can create their own best responses.

Recent research studies make clear that for adoptees the importance of adoptive issues is not limited to the moment of "the telling" but tends to become more insistent over the years. At each stage of development, from infancy to adulthood, there are new emotional and cognitive challenges for the adopted child to deal with. Moreover, the fact of adoption colors many other issues, such as autonomy, discipline, and developing sexuality. This book utilizes hundreds of interviews with adoptive parents and adult adoptees, as well as the leading studies of psychology, social work, and sociology, to present a variety of ways of thinking about the ongoing process of communication within the adoptive family. The important thing to remember is that there is always the opportunity to try again, to re-address the issues, to say "the right thing." Speech itself is the means by which parents can guide and help a child, the tool they can use to create a strong and healthy family bond—the way they can fulfill their own best intentions.

COMMUNICATING WITH
THE ADOPTED CHILD

1 Chosen or Ordinary

It is the nature of parents to want to believe their children are special. At one level, this is always true: each child is a unique being, and therefore uniquely lovable. At another level, this cherished parental belief is usually false. No matter how talented Liza is at drawing bunnies, or how serious Charlie looks when he sits down to do his math homework, at bottom they are pretty much like all the other children in their class, play group, or neighborhood. In fact, it is lucky for parents that most children are ordinary kids. They go through the same developmental stages, have the same range of thoughts and feelings, and end up as adults, ready to take on the similar challenges of love and work and responsibility. Even their problems, such as the temper tantrums of the Terrible Twos, or the teenage experimentation with drugs or disobedience, are shared by most of their age mates. In the same way, their parents are able to share their own discoveries about how to deal with these problems or turn to the advice of their generation's authorities on child-raising. Truly being different is a burden few people really want, or can handle. To be ordinary is to stand on the ground that has been satisfying to humanity since time immemorial.

With some justification, adoptive parents have a tendency to cling to a view of their child as "special". Unlike children raised in biological families, their child has been "chosen". Adoptive parents deliberately opt to take a particular child into the family, in contrast to biological parents, who simply rear the children born to them. The element of choice in adoption is underscored by the legally required period during which the child lives with the family before final adoption papers can be signed.

What Does It Mean to Be Chosen?

The idea of the specialness of their child, the connotation of "favored" that is attached to the word "chosen," expresses the gratitude and thankfulness of adoptive parents to their child for making possible the realization of their own dreams of being a family. Emphasis on the concept of special is also a way some adoptive parents convey their sympathy for a child who has had to suffer so early in life, and who so young has felt the impact of the inadequacy and suffering of others, the child's birth family.

But being "chosen" in this special way is a two-edged sword for the adoptee. At the same time that it may comfort and console, it also sets the child apart from others. What every child, adopted or not, needs and wants is to be ordinary. Any kind of special status, whether it is based on a physical handicap, an extraordinary talent, or the fact of adoption, can be felt as a hurt, and also a source of isolation from other children. To be ordinary is to be fully accepted, part of the group, ready to participate in all the social and cultural opportunities available.

Parents may mistakenly see the entitlements that come with "special" status as entirely positive. Extra attention may be lavished on the adopted child by parents and other adults. There may be a flow of gifts from the family, a constant emphasis on the child's abilities and talents, perhaps a reluctance ever to say no. The danger of this kind of specialness is that it makes it more difficult for the child to engage in the give and take that brings friendship and affection from others. Being "better" in this effortless way, without having to strive for it, effectively isolates a child. Moreover, to many adoptees, the special status is closely linked to a situation that once went radically wrong, even when what happened is not remembered. For them, being favored as special means having less than other children, not more. One adult adoptee remembered the pain of knowing that he was "chosen" only because he had earlier been given away. "How could that ever be good?" he asked sadly. Even though his adoptive parents loved him and he grew up in a good home, he still despised the label of "chosen."

The natural tendency of adoptive parents to make much of their children can thus be counterproductive. Adoptive parents can help their children most by remembering that it is the situation, not the child, that is out of the ordinary. The adopted child has the needs and desires common to all children, and the most basic of these is the deep sense of rootedness in the family. Adoptive parents who succeed in putting the issue of their child's specialness outside the daily life of the family say they find they need a firm resolve. "It takes focus," warn the Adamses, adoptive parents of Tommy and Jenny. Mr. Adams explains, "Even though our kids are special, the focus away from that attitude keeps self-consciousness away from the kids . . . us too, I suppose. We don't lose sight that we need to help Tommy and Jenny with certain issues, but most of the time we can forget about being an adoptive family and just be family." He might well have said, "regular family."

Can the Adopted Child Be an Ordinary Kid?

Is it really possible for the adopted child to be a "regular kid?" Adoptees face circumstances other children know nothing about. Some, for example, bear no physical resemblance to anyone else in their family. Others come into adoption when already past the early formative years and with personality patterns that do not mirror those of the adoptive family or the new culture in which they find themselves. And always there are the universal differences of adoption: the young child's challenge of understanding and getting through the hurt it causes that the adoptive parents did not make oneself; the worry of the thought that being different in parentage from other children is somehow wrong; the sadness of losing earlier attachments to the birth family or foster parents and the anxiety created by their seeming disappearance; the questions about the feelings, motivations, and circumstances of the birth parents.

Do these differences that adoptees must cope with as they grow up make becoming a "regular kid" more difficult? YES! The challenges inherent in growing up adopted demand an extra investment of emotional energy that most children are free to put solely into the universal tasks of growing up.

To become a reliable and responsible member of society, capable of both cooperation and self-reliance, every youngster must meet two types of challenge: the needs of one's inner self—that world of feelings and thoughts, self-judgments, aspirations and flights of imagination; and the demands of the outer world—the environment of people and things and places. Fortunate is the child who is able to take for granted the inner self, with its many needs and changes. The child who can get by with an average amount of emotional support from parents and other significant adults is able to direct most of his or her attention to mastering the demands of the environment. For most adoptees, it is not so easy to meet the needs of the inner self. The adoptive situation creates special circumstances, which in turn create special needs.

Thus adoptive parents are faced with a dilemma as they try to balance the special needs of the chosen child with the even greater need of that child to become a regular kid. They hope to raise their child to be resistant (or better yet invulnerable) to the hurts life metes out, for they feel their child has already gone through enough pain and loss. But it is not really possible for a child to be both ordinary and invulnerable. For *invulnerability is not an ordinary human trait.* Only legendary figures such as Superman or Little Orphan Annie can claim that quality. Interestingly, both are adoptees. They mirror the popular fantasy that adoptees are indeed special. It seems that society itself longs to confine the adoptee in a make-believe mold.

Human beings, incapable of true invulnerability, must settle for the gift of being able to bounce back after misfortune, of being able to heal the broken bone or the emotional hurt. A child's psychological strength and the later adult maturity that signifies one can give back more to life than demand from it, is always conditional. Such strength depends on many factors. One is the genetic heritage. Another is a successful traversing of the developmental rites of passage, especially learning to let go of the wish for total closeness to mother (the cardinal need of early emotional life) and establishing one's own identity (the cardinal sign that the end of adolescence has been reached).

Being adopted tends to sensitize a youngster early to the problems of growing up that all children must face sooner or later. One such problem is understanding what it means to be a part of a family. An example of how deep the struggle is to feel a part of a new family can be seen in the behavior of Angela, adopted at age six. A year later, she still refused to don the blue jeans and polo shirts common to other girls in her suburban neighborhood, but insisted on continuing to wear the kind of frilly, flounced dresses that had been the choice of her foster mother. Angela also made it clear that she didn't want to play on the swings and slides with her more exuberant peers. Mostly she chose to play alone, feeding her beloved dolls and creating games of make-believe around them. Her adoptive mother felt frustrated and embarrassed. She was a failure in her own eyes because she could not change her daughter's behavior, which was regarded by other mothers as too passive and out of step with the norm.

Eventually, Angela's mother realized that she was pressing the girl to conform to an Anglo ideal of behavior, while the child had been brought up by a loving Hispanic foster mother in a different tradition. Through her play, Angela had been struggling with her feelings about letting go of her first attachments, not only to the foster mother but to the culture in which she had been raised. Basically, the child's behavior was a good omen for the future. Although it gave pain to her new family for a time, it meant that Angela had a depth of loving feelings that she would eventually be able to transfer to them and their culture, as she slowly responded to their sustained love and care. In the meantime, Angela's mother learned to become companionable on the child's own terms, by joining in Angela's make-believe games. She found an old doll's tea set in the attic, dusted it off, and then helped her daughter throw lavish doll tea parties, working with her to create delicious pretend food and even new party costumes made from colored tissue paper. Thus she supported her child in bridging the gap from past to present. And her behavior was deeply satisfying to her daughter, because joining in with a child's play is always interpreted as a sign of caring.

The Role of Communication

Whatever challenges they face, adoptive parents do not need to be Superparents to help their child reach out for the goal of being a regular kid. Ordinary parental devotion, the compulsive yet unheralded need to put one's child's interests first, should be enough. It helps to be able to accept pain as a part of life, and to realize that the search for perfection makes solving problems harder. It also helps to be familiar with the particular interests of adopted children as they grow and change. Most important is the knowledge of how and when to use family conversation to comfort, to support emotionally, and to inform about the issues of adoption.

Research indicates that adoption is almost always deeply positive, a life and health-giving force in the child's life. Even under unusual circumstances, the kind that demand extra efforts by the parents to help their child adjust, adoption works well. Oddly, the very studies that show the beneficial effects of adoption also point to the one lack common to many adoptive families: a communication gap about the issues of adoption. And it does not seem to get better even as the adoptee matures. Adoptive parents confide that they never like to bring up the unique adoptive issues that impact their family. They say they would feel "too clumsy," would not know how to "answer well" the questions the child might ask. Similarly, the children hesitate to bring up their questions and concerns, or to disclose the characteristic themes threaded through their more usual interests, for fear of upsetting or embarrassing their parents.

Though the bonds of communication unite members of all families, in the biological family, communication is not the only bond. The Biblical lines, "Bone of my bones and flesh of my flesh," are used to symbolize the biological link between parent and child. But that flesh and bone link is absent in adoptive families. The members have only communication to forge their bonds and create a unit all can depend on. That is why communication is so important in the adoptive family. That's what this book is about.

Communication Informs and Comforts

Many parents tend to think of communication as limited to the process of conveying intellectual information. They judge their own ability to communicate in terms of whether or not their child picks up the information they intended to impart. For example, the aunt of two bright little boys tells the story of how the three-year-old biological son in the family was joined with his four-year-old adopted brother in a shared confusion about the term "adopt." In this family, the parents had used the word freely ever since they adopted their son, shortly after his birth. So at four, he sometimes spoke of himself to friends and relatives as "dopted." His younger brother would always hasten to add, "Me too! Me too!" and the older child then supported the younger's assertion.

The conscientious parents of these boys were dismayed when they realized their careful explanations about the differences in the way each son had come into the family had not been grasped by either son. What the parents failed to realize was that although their communication had not yet been received on the intellectual level, it had already succeeded on the emotional level. Even though the boys didn't understand adoption, they both felt comfortable about the issue. And because it was a subject they felt free to discuss, they did of course finally grasp it intellectually. When the older boy was ready to understand, his brother quickly followed suit. (As in so many families, the younger child seemed to learn at an earlier age than the older, perhaps because of the increased intellectual stimulation provided by the older child.) After that, the younger boy only said he wished he was adopted. The older son was proud to realize that his brother looked up to him and wanted to emulate him in every way—although in this particular case, obviously he could not.

The parents of these boys, like many of the parents interviewed for this book, feared that the answers they gave their curious children about adoption were not really satisfactory from an intellectual point of view. However, many of the adoptee's questions spring from the need common to all children to feel totally grounded in their family relationships. Thus, even if the initial telling is handled in a way the parents see as less than perfect, there is no need for despair. Parents can return to the subject many times, each time giving the child comfort and reassurance, along with information that will eventually correct mistaken impressions. In fact, an unhurried process of family talk about the complexities of adoption should continue into the teen years, at the youngster's own initiative and pace. In a family that gives members the freedom to say what is on their minds and in their hearts, children do express both intellectual questions and the feelings associated with the queries. Parents can plug into the power of speech to convey emotional support and encourage intellectual activity. This fortunate phenomenon, that the same words can simultaneously present an idea and express a feeling, is a major theme of this book.

In a family that gently encourages conversations about adoptive issues, a child learns by the example of the parents. Over time, the child acquires important skills: knowing how to talk about confusions rather than simply reacting to them, for example by having a temper tantrum; how to seek information actively rather than passively, as by trying to overhear a conversation among adults; and how to talk about one's own painful feelings, rather than denying their existence. When parents do not set an example in using speech to inform and comfort, there is often an effect on the child. A youngster may invest too much energy in exaggerated daydreaming and worrying about the unknown. A child may feel suspicious, sensing secrets within the family, wondering what they may be. Older children sometimes find it harder to concentrate in school, and their intellectual curiosity may be repressed for the same reasons.

Parents who know how to talk about adoptive issues in a way that is both supportive and informative are enablers to their children. They enable their youngster to devote more energy to the usual tasks of growing up, to be free of excessive concerns about adoption—and to reach out confidently for the coveted banner of the "regular kid."

Questions and Answers

One way to start thinking about the power of speech within the family is to look at the following questions about adoptive issues, all of them actual queries posed to their parents by real children. Each question is followed by five possible answers a parent could give. None of the answers is wrong, but some of them do raise some important issues about the way parents can simultaneously inform and comfort their children. Think about the effects of these various communications about subjects that are important in the adopted family; you may want to put a check by the answers you think you would feel most comfortable giving your own child. In the last chapter of the book, we will come back to these questions and answers, and talk about some of their implications.

1. Mrs. Gardner is undressing three-year-old Jimmy, preparing him for bed. Obviously not yet ready to go to sleep, the boy has been interrupting her constantly. From out of the blue he asks, "Did my 'other' mother give me a toy when I was very little? If she did, I want it!"

_____ **A.** I am sure your "other mother" gave you a toy.

_____ **B.** It's time for a good little boy to stop asking questions and go to bed.

_____ **C.** You have lovely toys now, so it shouldn't matter.

_____ **D.** Of course you are curious about things you don't remember.

_____ **E.** I don't know, I would have to find out for you. I'll call your social worker in the morning and ask.

2. Ten-year-old Skye looks away from the family TV and fidgets for a while. Then she asks, "Even if I knew my natural mother's name and where she lives, I don't want to see her. She probably has a family now. What would she want to see me for?"

_____ **A.** Of course, you never have to see her. But you might change your mind when you are older.

_____ **B.** Yes, your natural mother probably has a family now, and is sure and confident that you are loved and happy.

_____ **C.** You're right, children don't need to worry about make-believe. You've been with us so long, I am your real parent.

____ **D.** Okay, if you don't want to see her, you don't have to. Just think about the family and the love you have now.

____ **E.** You are wondering about what your natural mother is doing now. It's okay to think about her.

3. Mark is six years old. He is sitting at the dinner table with a dreamy look on his face. While everyone else eats, he plays with his fork. Then he starts to talk about what his "other" mother was like. He asks, "What was *her* mommy and daddy like—I'm thinking about all of them."

____ **A.** I don't know. Anyway, you are with us now, and we think you are special.

____ **B.** You'd like to know all about your other family and what their lives were like when they were children like you.

____ **C.** I really can't answer your questions. Maybe when you are older, we can find out the answers together.

____ **D.** Your "other" mother was a terrific person, and your biological grandparents were probably a lot like your adoptive grandparents.

____ **E.** I don't know about them. But a child doesn't need more than one family, and you know all about us and our parents.

4. Eight-year-old Kate, dressed for school, is sitting at the kitchen counter waiting for her mother to finish packing her lunchbox. She talks about being at a friend's house the previous afternoon, and how her friend looks just like her older sister. Kate asks, "Why can't I look like somebody besides just me, too?"

____ **A.** You'd like it if we looked like a family. But we are a family anyway.

____ **B.** You probably look like your biological family, the way your friend looks like hers.

____ **C.** You are much loved, and that is more than lots of biological children could say for themselves.

____ **D.** It isn't important for a child to resemble anybody in the family physically. Lots of children don't.

____ **E.** You are a very special person. You just look good by yourself.

5. Linda is helping her mother take the dishes out of the dishwasher and put them away. The eight-year-old suddenly asks, "Why didn't I come out of your stomach? Why couldn't I have?"

____ **A.** It would have been nice, but you came to me in a special kind of way.

____ **B.** If you had come out of me, then you wouldn't be gorgeous, like your natural mother.

____ **C.** Because that's the way God wanted it.

____ **D.** It doesn't matter where you come from but how much you are wanted, and we love you very much.

____ **E.** You wonder if maybe you are really my natural child after all, and feel you'd like to know all about your birth.

6. Eight-year-old David looks up from the homework he is doing, then asks his adoptive mother a question. "Why does it still hurt that my natural mother had me and then gave me up?"

___ A. I don't know . . . she gave you up because she wanted you to have a good home, like ours.

___ B. It's not necessary for children to think about these things, and then they don't get hurt.

___ C. I don't really know, but I have you now, and I'm sure glad, because I love you very much.

___ D. You're feeling sorry right now that you don't know her, or see her.

___ E. It might always hurt. It is a very tough experience to go through.

7. Andrea Johnson and her nine-year-old Margie look very different from one another. On a week-long vacation in a rented beach house, they go into a grocery store to buy food for dinner. Margie covers her face with the hood of her jacket; when her mother tells her not to do that, the girl answers defiantly, "I want to." She explains that people are staring at her because she looks so different from her mother. She adds that she thinks the other shoppers know she is not "from" her mother. "Why can't I cover my face?" she asks.

___ A. Children can't read people's minds. What these people in the grocery store think doesn't matter anyhow.

___ B. You have nothing to be ashamed of, because you are loved as much as anyone's children can be loved.

___ C. You are wondering what people think about us being together.

____ **D.** People can look different, like flowers are different.

____ **E.** Don't cover yourself up . . . maybe the other people here would like to get to know you.

8. Ten-year-old Matthew comes home from school and complains that the other children are teasing him because he is adopted. "How can I get them to stop?" he asks.

____ **A.** Life is like that. All children get teased sometimes. I'll talk to their parents, or you can handle it on your own.

____ **B.** Tell them how special you are because you were chosen. They weren't chosen, they were just born.

____ **C.** You're mad at the other kids for teasing you and frustrated because they don't stop. Maybe you are having trouble explaining to them what being adopted means.

____ **D.** If you don't appear to get upset at the teasing, they will get tired of it, I think.

____ **E.** Try not to let it bother you, because people only tease someone they like.

9. Eleven-year-old Ronny is supposed to be cleaning his room, but he is dawdling. When his father reminds him he needs to finish his task, Ronny says, "I used to be very embarrassed to be adopted." Then he asks, "Do you know why?"

____ **A.** Be proud, Ronny. Children are generally proud to be adopted.

____ **B.** It doesn't really matter, a lot of children are adopted.

___ **C.** Just think, we picked you out because we wanted you.

___ **D.** Perhaps you still feel that way and don't like that feeling.

___ **E.** When you aren't sure it is okay to be a certain way, you can feel embarrassed.

10. Twelve-year-old Vincent is putting a dimmer switch on the light fixture over the dining table. He turns to his adoptive parents and asks, "How come I am so handy, when you both are not?"

___ **A.** It's God's will that some children can do things and some cannot. It has nothing to do with how we are.

___ **B.** We are the lucky ones to have you around. Just imagine what it would be like here if you weren't around to help us out.

___ **C.** You have a gift for fixing things, and it is important to you.

___ **D.** You inherited some talents from your natural parents and perhaps you just developed your handiness on your own.

___ **E.** You're just really a terrific kid—what can I say?

2 Timing the Telling Moment

"I've thought a lot about what I want to say to Chris," confides one adoptive mother, watching her toddler trying to put one block on top of another. "I just don't know when I ought to say it."

The importance of the initial revelation that the child is adopted, often called the telling, is twofold. It gives the adoptee a critical piece of information that he or she is entitled to hear. It also lays the foundation for years of ongoing family discussions about the unique issues of adoption that arise as the adoptee passes through the sequence of developmental stages. For many parents, the hardest part about communication in the adoptive family is that decision about WHEN to start discussing the complex issues of adoption. The right timing of the telling is a source of anxiety to many parents.

The fact that expert opinion on this question is divided doesn't make it any easier for parents to make a decision. Although the study of child development has been going on throughout the twentieth century, it is only recently that researchers have focused on understanding how a child's capacity to know and understand the world develops. Such studies are difficult to do since they involve arranging some way to watch an ordinary child almost continuously without influencing the child in the process. They are usually based on a small number of cases and a sampling that is anything but random. For example, the landmark studies in child development by Swiss psychologist Jean Piaget, the foundation of much of the discipline, were almost entirely based on his observations of a single child, his own daughter. It may never be possible to gather enough evidence to be sure exactly how a young child develops the capability of understanding about complex issues like adoption. And the very fact that there is presently so much confusion about this question indicates that even once the general mechanism and timetable are understood, there will always be a significant range of individual variation.

The only consensus among the conflicting advice from the experts seems to be the worrisome conclusion that choosing the wrong moment can be harmful. This arouses a great deal of anxiety in adoptive parents about the decision. How can you know when it is the right time to open family communication about adoptive concerns?

An Early Telling

"I don't remember when we first told Petey," commented Alice. "I'm sure it was before he could really understand what it meant . . . in early infancy, I suppose. He heard the word 'adopted' along with 'Mommy' and 'Daddy.' Even if we accomplished nothing else, at least he was familiar with the sound of the word."

Like Alice, some parents prefer to make the adoptive situation a part of family communication from the very beginning of the child's life in the family. Although the infant cannot understand what is being communicated, it becomes integrated into the family environment. No decision about when to tell need ever be made, for the telling is continuous. As the child develops the ability to understand more clearly what being adopted means, he or she will pose additional questions that can gradually lead to fuller explanations. The child will probably never remember any single moment of telling, but rather will experience a gradual unfolding of the complicated emotional and intellectual issues of adoption.

An advantage of an early telling that seems important to many adoptive parents is that it insures their child will hear about being adopted from them, rather than from someone else. When the revelation comes early, around the time the child is three or four, there is little chance that the child will accidentally hear the facts of adoption from a friend or relative. So an early telling safeguards the child's trust and confidence in the parents. Mrs. O'Dell, an adoptive grandmother, spoke about how upset her grandson Tim had been when his adoption was inadvertently revealed to him by his aunt. He was nearly eight years old at the time. His parents had intended to tell him sooner, but for one reason or another they kept putting it off. "They said time just slipped by so quickly for them," said Mrs. O'Dell softly. "But it was such a shock for Tim. He couldn't forgive them for a long time."

Many adoptive parents find that sometime between the ages of three and five is the most comfortable time for them to make the first revelation to their child about the adoption. Few elect to introduce the idea quite as early as Alice and her husband did. "We tried it for a while when the baby first came and then dropped the practice," said Tina. "It seemed like it was wasted effort. Cindy couldn't comprehend the word, so why should we have to think about trying to use it all the time? We decided we would just relax and enjoy being a family. Telling Cindy about adoption could come later." It is more common for couples to begin introducing the word when their child is a toddler. At that stage, children are already able to use simple words and even some word strings. They can mouth the word "adopt." How much do they understand? It's an individual matter, depending on the child's own developmental path, but it does seem that some toddlers can in a minimal way understand the concept of two mothers before their third year, and even appear to be comfortable with the implications.

A Late Telling

But what is most comfortable for the parents is not necessarily the best for the child. Recently, several noted psychoanalysts (among them the late Lili Peller and Herbert Wieder) have advised that parents should wait until the child is at least older than five. Their experience in treating adopted children has convinced them that when the revelation comes before the child achieves a certain degree of emotional and intellectual maturity, it creates intellectual confusion and unsettled feelings.

To learn that one is adopted can be a tremendous blow to a child's self-esteem. Giving away a child is, after all, a very adult concept, not part of a child's view of the world. Children do not give away something they treasure, and it is hard for them to understand that adults may have many valid reasons for such an unselfish action. Young children cannot understand that the birth parents who gave them away could care about them— that the very fact of adoption is a sign of the birth parent's love and care.

For adoptive children, finding out that there is no biological tie to the adoptive family is equally hurtful. It's as if something is wrong with them and with the adoptive parents too. The younger the child at the time of the telling, the more likely it is that he or she will react by feeling insecure about belonging to the family, or perhaps even to view the family itself as lacking in security.

But what about the danger that the child will hear about the adoption from someone else? One reason many parents choose to make the revelation as early as the child's third or fourth year is their worry that a well-meaning relative or friend will let slip a reference to adoption. As the child grows older, and has more and more exposure to the world outside the home, such an accidental revelation grows more and more likely. Parents also worry about unintentionally cruel teasing by other children who have heard about the adoption before their own child knows the facts, and fear that a late telling leaves their child too vulnerable. Once a child reaches school age, the difficulties of keeping adoption a secret multiply. Thus parents may feel pressured into telling their child sooner than they consider ideal, because they want to make sure the child hears of the adoption from them rather than from others. One comfort for parents in this situation is that the young child who hears the revelation from others does not lose trust in the parents. Generally, the child of two or three who learns from someone else that he or she is adopted does not grasp the full meaning of the statement and will immediately turn to the parents for help in understanding it. That gives parents the opportunity to deal with the situation in their own way, as part of the long-term communication process within the family that helps their child master the complex physical and emotional realities of adoption.

Some experts who favor a late telling suggest that parents simply deny the story if their youngster comes to them after hearing it elsewhere. A child is much more likely to believe the parents' denial than the manifestly confusing story heard from someone else. According to this line of reasoning, if the subsequent telling is handled well, the discovery that the parents have told a white lie will do minimal damage to the child's trust. Intuitively, most parents are reluctant to test the validity of this theory.

In making a decision about when to begin the life-long process of family communication about adoptive issues, there are really two overlapping issues. One is the child's trust in the word of the parents. The other is the child's sense of being wanted and of belonging securely to the family. Unfortunately, protecting a child's trust by a very early telling can be upsetting to the child's feelings about being unconditionally wanted. That is a dilemma no one can tell an adoptive parent how to solve neatly.

The Child's Readiness

Ideally, parents should give the information when a child reaches a certain level but not beyond—like a chocolate pudding that is firming but has not yet formed a surface skin. The child who learns too early may experience a loss of self-esteem and a diminution of the feeling of secure belonging within the family. The child who is informed too late, say as old as ten, seems to take it even harder than the little ones. The older child feels deeply betrayed and is harder to comfort. It all comes down to understanding a child's readiness. If a child is ready at four years to hear about being adopted, by all means talk about it. But some children might need more time to mature before they can make sense of the complicated issues of adoption, or can deal with the emotions the revelation will arouse. They might need to wait for an additional year, or even two, before the telling.

How can you tell when your child is ready? There are some guidelines that can help you assess your child's emotional maturity, as you make the important decision about how to time the telling. The following questions focus on some keys to readiness.

1. Is your child comfortable with being away from you for hours at a time, while attending school or playing with other kids?
2. Can your child sleep without a light on?
3. Does your child sometimes visit a friend or relative overnight?
4. Does your child have a pet? Can the child take responsibility for the pet's care?
5. Has your child learned how to keep a secret?
6. Can your child follow a logical discussion?
7. Does your child have a sense of time? Can he or she distinguish the present from the past or the future?

If you can answer "yes" to most of the questions, then your child is probably ready to hear the revelation of adoption.

A child who is able to leave home for extended periods already feels confident about belonging to the family. The secure child has a permanent picture of home in the back of the mind, an inner conviction that the loving family will always be there and that his or her place there is as constant as Old Glory waving in the breeze. That child can go out into the world alone, to participate in a play group or to stay overnight with grandparents, because the invisible security of the family is continually present. Being able to sleep without a light on is another sign of a child's trust in the family's security, an absolutely necessary precondition for revealing the facts of adoption.

Another factor of readiness is a child's ability to be kind to other people and to behave responsibly toward them. Children who enjoy taking care of a pet are more able to imagine how their parents feel, including the distress of birth parents who could not keep and care for their own child, and the wish of adoptive parents to have a child to care for and the pleasure they receive in doing it. Children who can take on a nurturing role with their pet can begin to understand the parental motivations of the adults involved in the adoptive situation.

The child who can keep a secret has developed a sense of self-control, a sense of the boundaries of things. A secret is almost like a family possession, something that belongs only to the family and not to outsiders. A secret is also something that makes "our family" unique, separate from all others. The child who keeps a secret can take pride in protecting the family's uniqueness.

Being an adoptive family then becomes another aspect of the family's uniqueness. Knowing how to keep a secret is not only a sign that the child is emotionally ready to learn about adoption, but also has a practical application. It means the child will be able to use judgment as to when to disclose the adoption to others outside the immediate family. Adoption, for all its public aspect, remains a private matter.

The final factor of readiness is the child's intellectual comprehension. Between the years of six and eight, children take a great leap forward in their general ability to comprehend. An eight-year-old's thinking is more like an adult's than like a nursery-school child's, although the age difference might make you think otherwise. The school-age child can follow a logical discussion and has a realistic sense of time, based on an ability to differentiate the present from the past and the future. A child of six, seven, or eight is no longer totally dependent on adults for guidance in making decisions. During those years, the child begins to make personal judgments and to evaluate what is good and what is not. That child is ready to think about adoptive issues and come to a conclusion like, "It is good to be adopted and be part of my family."

There are three specific issues of intellectual comprehension that should be established before a child is ready for learning about adoption. They are:

1. The concept of the family unit to which the child belongs;
2. The recognition that families, and individuals, exhibit differences; and

3. An understanding of human reproduction and
   birth.

The first perspective, the concept of belonging to the
family, unites the child to the adoptive parents and
creates a sense of belonging. To hear that "we are an
adoptive family" has a good ring to it, a sense of comfort
in the belonging. In contrast, the notion that "you are an
adopted child" makes the adoptee feel isolated, singled
out, separated from the rest of the family. Thus the
concept of belonging to a family, and experiencing things
together, is an important foundation for the communication process about adoption.

The idea that children belong to their families does
not have to be taught, for it is part of the natural knowledge of childhood. But parents can expand that idea of
belonging in ways that will prepare the child to understand adoption, and to view it in the context of the
comfort and security of being a part of a family. That
will lead to establishing a second perspective that is
necessary before the telling: recognizing that people, and
families, exhibit differences.

Once a child has indicated an intellectual awareness
of the fact that there can be more than one type of any
particular thing—balls, flavors of juice, books for bedtime reading—parents can begin to introduce the information that there can be more than one kind of family.
(One good way to approach this topic is to read aloud
the book by Norma Simon, *All Kinds of Families*). There
is the family in which the children are all grown up, and
the family of a different race. There are the families of
nature: the bird family that lives in a nest high up in the
tree over the garage, the cat and her kittens who share

the house with the human family, the mother guppy and the new babies swimming in their fish tank. There are families with one child or many children, families with one parent or two. There are biological families and there are adoptive families. The child should become aware of the many different versions of the concept of family well before the telling takes place.

The third gentle step towards readiness for communication about adoption comes when the child displays some familiarity with the idea of the birth process itself. Children are ready to learn about this topic when they start to notice and ask about the names of their body parts and functions, and about the differences between boys and girls. Questions such as "Where did I come from?", or "Why does my new baby brother look different from me?", are signs that the subject can be introduced by parents. It is best to follow the cues given by the child, to answer in simple and accurate language, and to answer only the question that is asked rather than adding other related information.

When Justin was two, he asked his mother why boys urinate differently from girls. He was not asking for information about sexuality, a concept in which he was not yet interested. He was simply concerned about the differences he had observed in the functioning of a little boy's body and a little girl's body. It was the difference itself that he wanted to know about, because he was at the age of learning about the world through the concepts of similarity and difference. Justin's mother wisely offered the answer that little girls and little boys urinate differently because they are made differently. As it happened, that was enough to satisfy the boy's curiosity at that age. If he had shown signs of not being fully satisfied by that answer, his mother might have added the information that the differences are there so that little boys can grow up to be fathers and little girls can grow up to be mothers. That type of answer tells a child that the story is to be continued later, as appropriate.

Parents often notice that a child seems to lose interest once a question has been answered, no matter how important the subject. That loss of interest is perfectly normal. Children have a short attention span. Moreover, their focus is not the same as an adult's, so they are not interested in details and specifics that an adult might consider important. Often, it is apparent by a child's reaction that a "complete" answer to a question is more than he or she bargained for. Taking the cue from the child's interest will give the right direction to the parent's answer. Information can be given in small doses. If the child does not persist in questioning, the parent should stop, without offering further elaboration.

The Holding Environment

The single most important issue in an adopted child's readiness to deal with the telling is the sense of being wanted by and belonging to the family. This feeling gets its start in the environment created by the adoptive mother. The renowned English psychoanalyst, D. W. Winnicott, gave this the name "holding environment," meaning that it creates a safe and embracing place in which a child can grow and develop.

From the very beginning, an infant becomes attached to its mother by repeatedly experiencing pleasure at her hand and the beginnings of gratitude for it. Increasingly, the baby recognizes Mother's touch, the characteristic odor of her skin, the tone of her voice, and eventually her face. Each mother differs from all others in such things as the way she picks up her infant, the tempo of her response to her baby's cries, or the vigor of her rocking. A mother's individual approach to nurturing her infant constitutes that child's holding environment. A baby's holding environment is a complex physical and social experience that replaces the earlier physiological environment, the holding of the womb.

A comparison of two adoptees, Dorothy and Felicity, helps illustrate the importance of the holding environment in making a child ready to learn about adoption. Dorothy's birth mother was an unmarried nurse, who lived in a large northeastern city. She told her social worker that her pregnancy was the result of a "mistake," but she did not believe in abortion. She made arrangements through a lawyer to find adoptive parents (in the same city) for her child. After an uncomplicated pregnancy and easy delivery, the birth mother saw Dorothy once and then placed the baby in the arms of her adoptive mother on the day she left the hospital.

From the start, Dorothy thrived. At six months, she showed the characteristic developmental reaction called "stranger anxiety," the temporary rejection of everyone except the mother. That meant Dorothy was clearly aware of her mother as a special person. Earlier in her life, Dorothy had only needed mothering; now she needed a particular mother. A child who has never desired mother so deeply as to reject all others (if only for a brief period) can never feel really wanted or desirable. Eventually, a child's wish for a particular loving mother flowers into the conviction of being wanted by her in return.

In contrast to Dorothy's comfortable beginning in life, Felicity was born in dire circumstances. Her birth mother was a native of a Latin American country. The unmarried woman already had four children, and the family lived in poverty. Their only income was the low wage the mother earned by working long hours as a maid in a nearby town. The family home was a one-room, dirt-floored shack, without windows or running water. When this woman learned she was pregnant for the fifth time, she decided she would have to abandon the child she knew she could not care for. The birth mother confided this decision to the cook at the home where she worked, and through a long chain of contacts initiated by the cook, information about the situation finally reached the couple in the United States who would become the baby's adoptive parents.

Arrangements for the adoption were made when the birth mother was in her fourth month of pregnancy. To insure that the baby received adequate nutrition for its fetal development, the adoptive parents sent large quantities of powdered milk, canned foods, and vitamins—enough not only for the birth mother but for her four other children as well, so she would not be tempted to sacrifice her needs for theirs.

Felicity's birth was uneventful, and she was a healthy and normal baby. But because of bureaucratic complications she could not be taken immediately to her adoptive home. Thus Felicity remained with her birth family for about nine months, while the legal formalities were being processed.

During that time, the adoptive parents continued to send huge supplies of food to the family, and they visited several times to become acquainted with Felicity. They learned that the baby's birth mother had returned to work as soon as she was able, and (perhaps intentionally) she developed no attachment to the newcomer. The infant was cared for by an eight-year-old sister, who carried Felicity with her everywhere, strapped into a harness on her back. For the first months of her life, the circumstances of Felicity's life differed from those of the rest of her birth family in just one way: she slept alone, in the crib sent by her adoptive parents, while the others slept two or three together, on cots that jostled up against her crib.

When Felicity finally arrived in her new home, she experienced a complete change of physical surroundings. She had her own bedroom, and even her own bathroom. Her room was full of toys chosen to give her comfort and stimulate her senses, and she had a huge wardrobe of colorful and attractive clothes. Her every need was responded to by two eager adults.

Yet, much to the distress of her adoptive parents, Felicity did not do well in her new home. Her rate of weight gain was very slow, and her muscular development was poor. She cried constantly, day and night. Her despairing parents could not pinpoint what was wrong, and the specialists they consulted could not offer a definite answer. They learned from weary experience that the only comfort the baby seemed to respond to was being carried. She would nestle her head against her mother's or father's shoulder, and gain some measure of calm through the repeated movement. But when Felicity was put down, her crying started up immediately. For months, her parents took turns carrying Felicity ceaselessly, until both appeared utterly exhausted.

It took about six months before Felicity started to change for the better. She gained weight, her physical development spurted forward, and she was finally able to be on her own without crying. Soon she began to show anxiety with strangers, and her wish to be close to her adoptive mother was manifest. Felicity had finally made the leap and become deeply attached to her new family.

It seemed ironic to her adoptive parents that Felicity had taken so long to adjust to their love and comfort; in fact, she had actually fared better in her emotionally and materially deprived birth environment than she did when she first arrived in her new home. But it is not hard to understand the family's experience if one realizes that, in her birth home, Felicity had become attached to her own special holding environment—the care of her sister and the feeling of the back harness that transmitted the warmth of the older girl's body and the motion of her activity.

In contrast to Felicity, Dorothy's psychological development moved ahead smoothly within the context of an unbroken holding environment, like a seedling in the protection of a cold frame. Her experience was about as close to that of the child in a biological family as is possible in the circumstances of adoption. Thus Dorothy did not need the protection of the holding environment as long as Felicity did. Felicity experienced a sharp break in the holding environment established in her birth family. What that meant to her psychologically was a hurt that had to heal before her development could start up again. Self-healing is no small task for an infant. That it could happen at all attests to the resilience of Felicity's spirit, and the powers of nurturance of her adoptive family.

Clearly, Dorothy will be ready to learn about adoption at an earlier age than Felicity, because she will be ready to leave the security of her adoptive family's holding environment sooner. Felicity's parents would be well advised to wait until the little girl shows every sign of readiness.

Parents Need Confidence, Too

One last factor in selecting the optimal time for the telling should be emphasized. Communication is always a two-way street, so both parties must be ready for the process to begin. Just as the child should be psychologically ready, so should the parents. According to those who work professionally with adoptive families, many parents, including mental health professionals who are adoptive parents themselves, worry about what to say and when to say it. Although it is natural to be concerned about an important milestone in the family's experience, much of the worry about the telling is needless.

In fact, worrying too much about the telling is likely to be counterproductive. As Don and Nancy discovered, the more relaxed the parents are about conveying the information, the more likely it is that the child can understand and accept it. Adoptive parents of two children, they recalled that their older child went through a prolonged period of confusion about the issue, whereas their younger child had an easier time handling their explanations. Commented Don ruminatively, "I think we might have been more relaxed the second time round. You learn from your experience—and your mistakes—with the first one. Looking back on it, I think we probably confused Teddy, our first child . . . maybe we were trying too hard."

What really matters is keeping the process of communication going, continuing to use the power of speech to inform and comfort over the long years of the child's development. Adoptive communication is a powerful tool for parents who know how to use it.

3 Once Told Is Not Enough

"Adoption" is a complex concept. It includes factual matters, such as the existence of two sets of parents, and the change from the birth environment to a new one, that may be difficult for a child to grasp. It also carries an emotional charge, not only in regard to the adoptee's own feelings about the events of the past, but also in the child's attempt to understand the feelings of the adults involved in the adoptive situation. A child's ability to grasp the facts and feelings of adoption and remain comfortable about them is successful mastery. Adoptive parents can help their child achieve that mastery by gently preparing the child for hearing about the adoption, and by giving a simple but straightforward explanation of the adoption at the appropriate time.

The way a child masters any complex idea is to take it in small pieces, which usually need to be repeated frequently. Eventually, all the small building-blocks of information will be fitted together to create a complete version of the complex idea. Thus, telling a child about adoption is not a one-time event, but rather an ongoing process of communication between adoptive parents and child that may literally take years before the entire complex concept is mastered. No single conversation—whether handled well or poorly—is as important as the adoptive parents' commitment to the long-term communication process. A family environment of easy communicating about ideas and feelings provides a good head start for the simple and repetitive conversations that will help a child master the concept of adoption.

Children have individual ways of integrating new information. To "forget" and later ask the same question so as to elicit the same answer is one common approach to mastering new information. When a child repeats a question several hours, or days, later, it is appropriate to repeat the very same answer. Other children may remember the earlier conversation and ask for further information much later. At that time, additional details can be given, in the same small doses. The best guideline: Answer ONLY the question the child is asking, in the simplest possible way.

Unnecessary explanations can cause unnecessary problems. For example, when five-year-old Jeffrey asked his father, "Why are my eyes blue when yours and Mommy's are brown?", he was not looking for an explanation of the principles of genetics, although that might be appropriate for an older child who has begun to be interested in a scientific point of view. Nor did it imply that Father must immediately inform Jeffrey that he was adopted. The question arose from Jeffrey's observation that family members often have the same eye color, and that was the issue—and the only issue—he was addressing.

A good way for Father to handle the question would have been to start by praising Jeffrey for his powers of observation, and talking about examples of families they know in which everyone has the same eye color. Then the topic could be extended to mention the fact that in many families, people have different eye colors. (Of course, this is true in biological families as well as adopted ones.) For many children, that would be a sufficient response.

As it happened, Jeffrey persisted in asking his original question: why was theirs one of the families in which people had different eye colors instead of the same? His father answered, "In some families, children do look different from their families. There are some reasons for it, but it is too soon for me to explain it to you now. We'll talk about it again when you are eight." The answer was candid, although incomplete in the factual sense. It satisfied Jeffrey. He had reason to believe that a fuller answer to his question would follow in time, for his father had always been trustworthy.

Jeffrey forgot his question before long, but his father did not. Several years later, after Jeffrey had been informed that he was part of an adoptive family, his father reminded him of the earlier conversation and the fact that he was now due the full explanation. Jeffrey was pleased that his father remembered, and kept his promise. Even though he had forgotten the issue, his father's thoughtfulness was reassuring.

Finding Outside Support

Many parents find that outside support helps them through the process of communicating the concept of adoption. Their own parents, siblings, and close friends can of course provide meaningful encouragement, but in most cases, these people cannot offer the specific support and advice concerning adoptive matters that parents need. They usually lack previous experience with adoption, and thus cannot provide a role model for adoptive parents. However, a strong network is available through adoptive parents' groups, which can be found in most large cities. Regular meetings, both formal and informal, provide information, support, and the wisdom of collective experience.

The benefits of participation in an adoptive parents' group include direct help for the adopted child, even if the child has not yet been informed about the adoptive status. Group social activities, such as picnics in the summer and holiday parties in the winter, provide a pleasant environment in which a child can be gently introduced to the word "adopt" and its many implications. Through the mere fact of belonging to the group, the child can realize, "We are a family of adoption. We are having a nice time at our picnic, where we play, eat, and go swimming with other (adoptive) families."

One of the best features of this type of introduction to the concept of adoption is that there is no pressure on the child to respond. The child who is not ready to begin mastering the concept of adoption will not even notice that it is a theme of the gathering. The older child, the one who is already in the process of learning what adoption means, will signal the fact by questions—most likely about the social event itself, or the other families the child met there, rather than about the child's own specific status.

Frances and Barry, parents of two-year-old Elizabeth, agree that their adoptive parents' group has a lot to offer. "I particularly like the fact that it gives us a natural way to introduce the word 'adoption' to our daughter," says Barry. "It reminds me of living in a foreign country, like Frances and I did when we were first married. Americans who lived in Paris used to get together every year to celebrate the Fourth of July. It was a good party, and it was also a way to remember that we were Americans, and in that particular way different from the people we were living among." Barry sees the parallel between those Fourth of July parties and the social events sponsored by the adoptive parents' group. The gatherings can help daughter Elizabeth become aware of the word "adopted," just as she might become aware of the word "American." It will also help her recognize that adoption is one way that some families are different from others.

When the Time Is Right

When they are sure their child is ready, it is up to the parents to select an appropriate moment for the telling. It should be a time when everyone in the family is free, and there is nothing pressing on the schedule. The child does not have to go to school, the parents don't have to go to work or fix meals or prepare for guests arriving soon. It is a peaceful time—no jangling telephone or television that is competing for the family's attention.

Once parents have decided that it is time for the telling, they may find it difficult to bring the topic up out of the blue. Starting an explanation about the complex subject of adoption, a topic which has not yet been discussed by the family as a whole, may go more smoothly if it evolves from talking about a related subject. The child may ask a question that touches on the adoption issue that can be used to lead into the personal revelation. Jeffrey's question about eye color is an example, although five-year-old Jeffrey was not yet prepared for the telling and thus his father did not use it as a springboard for opening the subject. If no such opportunity is created by the child, the parents can introduce a related topic, such as the arrival of a new baby at the home of friends or family.

Another approach may be to use a book to bring up the subject and to convey some of the information. Reading a special book together as part of the telling allows each member of the family a way of getting a little distance from the emotions that the first presentation will arouse. The book will become a symbol of the event of the telling, and can be read again many times as part of the ongoing process of mastering the complex concept of adoption. One highly recommended book for this purpose is *Our Baby, An Adoption Story* by Janice Koch. Using an appropriate format and language, this book is addressed directly to the child. It uses simple accurate language to explain how the child was born and how the child came into the adoptive family.

Many stories for children refer directly or indirectly to the concept of adoption, and may be used as part of the preparation for the telling. According to psychologist Joan Fassler, an appropriate story gives a child information in a matter-of-fact way, does not overstimulate nor manipulate the imagination, and leaves room for the child to identify with the adoptee without demanding that response.

The heart of the telling is a statement like, "We needed a child to love and care for, and you needed a family to love and care for you." To parents, the telling may seem so momentous an occasion that they become very anxious about it. It may bring reassurance to remember that the event of telling is just one part in the process of communicating the intellectual and emotional aspects of adoption. The process began when the toddler first heard the word "adoption" and will continue well into the child's teens, as the youngster slowly masters more and more of the complex issue. If the initial telling is handled less than perfectly, there will be many opportunities to return to the subject, to correct mistaken impressions, and to give the child comfort and reassurance.

The Telling Moment

The telling unfolds a story of decisions and details that is of lifelong significance to the adoptee. It is a valuable and continuing chapter in the family history, to be viewed with respect and pride by adoptive parents and child alike.

Lucilla, the adoptive mother of Kevin and Linda, turned the telling into a story, one that took its place alongside such favorites as "Goldilocks" and the adventures of Pooh. "When Kevin was six and Linda was four, I sat down in the living room with one on either side of me. I took a deep breath and started out with, 'Once upon a time . . .'," Lucilla was launched on the telling.

"Once upon a time," she explained, "there was a lady and a man who wanted children, and they could not make the children by themselves. They wanted a boy first, so he could be a big brother and take care of his younger sister. There was a children's home close by, and so they went there and asked if they could have a little boy." The story continued with details of how the lady and the man met a little boy and wanted to take him right home. It described the tiny suit they bought for him to wear on the very first day they were a family. Then the story skipped ahead two years, to the time the lady and the man went back to the home to ask for a sister for the boy. "They saw a little girl with a lot of black hair and the most beautiful blue eyes, who was wearing a red dress, and they immediately wanted her to be part of their family." The story stressed how much the parents wanted both the children, and the great delight of the first meeting with each.

At the end of the story, Lucilla looked at her children and asked, "Do you know what the names of the little girl and the little boy are?" Of course they did, but they waited in happy anticipation for their mother to reveal the story's ending. "The lady and the man were Mommy and Daddy, and the little boy and the little girl are you!"

For Lucilla's children, the telling created a story that became part of their treasured family history, one they later named the story of "How You Got Us." Like all children, they liked reviewing the details of their beginnings. The adoptee's story is different, but the adopted child's feeling about it is not different.

Here are some guidelines for parents to bear in mind as they create their own family history through the telling.

1. Place the story in the context of the entire adoptive family. Adoption is not an event that happens only to the adoptee, but to the whole family. It is a story about "we," not about "you."
2. Tell the truth, as far as you know it and as far as the child can understand it. It is tempting to try to protect a child through untruths such as "Your parents died," or "Your mommy asked us to love you and take care of you." Whatever present comfort these untruths offer, they carry the risk that when the child is older and learns the truth, it will damage his or her trust in the adoptive parents.
3. Don't overload the child's imagination with too much information about the birth parents. At the time of the first telling, the child is not yet truly interested in the birth parents as individuals; it is enough just to integrate the idea that there are two sets of parents.
4. Present the action of birth parents in a positive light, for the adopted child needs to be able to take pride in his or her past. A good approach is to frame the reasons for giving up the child in terms of lack of competence. Those are reasons a child can understand, and they are true reasons.
5. It is not necessary to go into details about emotional, social, or economic reasons the birth parents were not competent to raise the child. A young child may be confused by the reasons, or see them from a different point of view. For example, a child who is told that the birth parents were "too young" to start a family has trouble comprehending that a parent could also be a

child, especially since to a young child, even teenagers seem grown up. This is a reason frequently
given the adoptee by parents, as some of the
stories in this book indicate.

6. No unsavory details about the birth parents
should be included in the early telling. A young
child is unable intellectually or emotionally to
deal with such concepts as mental illness, illegitimacy, or child abuse. Statements such as "The
lady who gave birth to you was mentally ill," or
"You were born in a prison," do not help the
adoptee, who needs to take pride in everything
connected with his or her beginnings in life. That
kind of information can be saved for the teen
years, and should be revealed only when the
youngster has a chance to understand some of
the circumstances that influence behavior in a
deviant direction.

7. Information about the adoptive parents' inability
to make children themselves should be given
matter-of-factly, without graphic details. An explanation like, "some couples cannot make a
baby" is enough at first.

8. Allow the child to interrupt the telling with questions as they arise, and answer each question
before continuing. If the child has to wait before
the story is finished, he or she may forget, or
decide not to ask, puzzling questions.

The Child's Response to the Telling

The way children react to the telling varies, and
parents should be alert for signs that a child needs

further help. Some adoptive parents report that their child responded with complete silence. For example, Marie said her son expressed no surprise when she told him, at the age of nine, that he was adopted, although his three younger sisters were not. Moreover, the boy never mentioned the subject again. Another troubling response may be an almost obsessive concern over the adoptive status. Arlene, informed at the age of four, never seemed to stop talking about adoption. Four years later, she was still introducing herself to strangers by saying, "Hello, I am Arlene. I am adopted." When children react in either of these extreme ways, their parents should consider the possibility that the child may be troubled in some way by the status.

More usually, the child will respond to the telling by asking questions—especially if the family is one in which talk is encouraged. The Wellers were that kind of family, and their son Ben was a questioning boy. In fact, his questions were so probing that Marybeth and Don often felt unsure of how to satisfy him. The Wellers had adopted Ben, who was black, when he was three months old. By the age of three, the observant little boy had already noticed that his skin color was not the same as his parents'. Knowing that he had also observed the difference between boys and girls, his parents led him step by step to understand the birth process and then to know that he was adopted.

Ben immediately had further questions for his mother. "Did I cry when I was born?" he wanted to know. "Of course you did," answered Marybeth. Ben persisted: "How do you know I did?" Unhesitatingly she responded, "Because all babies cry." Of course, she understood that he wanted her to say she had been a witness to his birth, but like most adoptive mothers, that was not the case. Marybeth didn't want to tell Ben a lie and thus set him up for a disappointment in her later, when he was old enough to realize she had no information about his behavior at birth. By giving a truthful but general answer, she was able to satisfy Ben's curiosity and at the same time give him a lesson in coping with one of the potentially unsettling mysteries of adoption, the blank in one's early history. She used logic to provide comfort.

Ben, obviously the kind of child who enjoys pondering life's weighty matters, continued to ask questions related to his adoption for several years. Usually, his parents felt that they managed to satisfy his desire to know and to give him emotional comfort. But, like all human beings, they sometimes failed. Marybeth later remembered one occasion in particular when she embarrassed herself by her response to one of Ben's questions.

It was a summer Saturday, and the lunch dishes had been cleared away. Don had taken Ben's younger sister, also adopted, and his mother out for a drive; Marybeth was sunning herself on the deck and idly thumbing a magazine. Ben, on his way to play with his friends, stopped to ask, "Why didn't God make it so boys have boy babies and girls have girl babies?" Before Marybeth could answer this tough question, he followed up with another: "And how was I born?"

All children learn by hearing information repeated many times over. The adopted child, trying to cope with the mystery of the missing record of one's own beginning in life, frequently seeks to master the idea, and reassure himself or herself about its meaning by asking questions.

Marybeth knew this, and so she dealt patiently with her son's repeated questions about reproduction and birth.

To give Ben some concrete answers, Marybeth turned to the encyclopedia. Together they sat for several hours, turning the pages and discussing the illustrations. Ben seemed particularly dumbfounded by a drawing of a fetus in the uterus, sucking its thumb. "Did I suck my thumb, too?" he wondered.

Marybeth answered, "I imagine you did, but nobody could really know, because nobody could see you." Ben's next question was about the color of his skin when he was a fetus. Was he already black then? His mother said she didn't know but she would ask the pediatrician and get an answer for him. They turned another page and Ben had another question. "When could I have inter-course?"

Marybeth knew her tone changed but she couldn't help feeling defensive. She found herself parrying her son's questions instead of answering them. "With inter-course comes a certain commitment," she said evasively. Ben shot back, "What does commitment mean?" Trapped, Marybeth responded, "it's responsibility . . . protecting . . . enjoying. . . ." Her voice trailed off in the characteristic way that tells a child the parent doesn't want to talk about it any more. But Ben refused to give up. He pointed out firmly, "I still don't understand com-mitment. What does it mean?"

By this time Marybeth felt flustered and decidedly inadequate. She tried to conclude the discussion by say-ing illogically, "When you are old enough to understand commitment, you'll be ready for intercourse." She knew the answer was wholly unsatisfactory to her son, who expected more of her than evasions and cover-ups. The tenacious little boy then reminded her, "You never answered my first question. Why didn't God make boys to have boy babies and girls to have girl babies?"

Marybeth gave up the attempt to answer any more of Ben's questions. "I really don't believe in God," she said, an answer that was truthful but not helpful to Ben. Sensing her desire to end the conversation, the puzzled boy went out to play with his friends. Marybeth was left with her feeling of embarrassment over her failure to handle Ben's questions. She felt even worse when Ben brought the subject up again at the dinner table and his grandmother handled it with ease. God arranged things in a certain way, the senior Mrs. Weller answered staunchly, "because He wants it that way." Ben had received an answer that satisfied him, and the subject was closed.

Although Marybeth was upset by her lapse, she could take comfort in the fact that Ben's questioning was really a sign of good parenting. The little boy was secure enough to persist in asking questions and confident enough to assume he could get what he wanted if he tried hard. The Wellers had given him the support and encouragement that allowed his curiosity to blossom.

Many adoptive parents have reported that the first question their child asks after the telling is why he or she was not born of the adoptive parents. Often, the question is put as though the child believes it was due to some choice made by the adoptive parents. There is usually a hint of disappointment underneath the question, a covert message that "right now, the world has let me down." The missing birth link seems to mean, "I am not 'at one' with mother." (The psychoanalytic author Louise Kaplan has written eloquently about the "at-one with mother" feeling.) A child may ask this question more than once. Especially when children are informed of their adoption before they can really grasp its complex meaning, they will return to this question.

Jeannette and Tom had informed their daughter Annie of her adoption when she was about two and a half years old, too young in many respects to master the concept. Later, not long after Annie's fifth birthday, she brought the troubling problem of the missing birth link up again. The little girl had spent a warm spring morning playing in the back yard next door with her friend Carrie, who had a new baby sister sleeping in a carriage on the patio. Annie clumped into the kitchen, where Jeannette helped her out of her muddy shoes and play clothes.

"Did I come out of your stomach, Mom?" asked Annie suddenly.

Jeannette was surprised to realize that the explanations she and Tom had previously given Annie about her adoption had not been sufficient. But she tried to remain as calm and undefensive as possible. "No, dear, you didn't," she answered.

The articulate little girl responded, "I feel sad, Mom. Why not?"

Jeannette answered from her heart. "I am sad, too, but I could not physically make a child. I wish you had come out of my stomach." Mother and daughter were momentarily silent, sharing this sad moment together. Then Jeannette smoothed Annie's hair and asked her, "Would you like to have some of Grandma's Christmas blueberry jam with cream cheese for lunch? There is some left that I have been saving." The blueberry jam was a particular favorite of Annie's, as it had been of

Jeannette's when she was her daughter's age. The loving link of family continuity helped both Annie and Jeannette feel better. Jeannette was relieved to see from her daughter's expression that she had been able to comfort her and help her through a difficult moment. Later, the mother reported, "I guess I could forgive myself at that moment for the fact that I had not physically made her."

Annie raised her disappointment that her mother had not given birth to her again from time to time because it was an important issue for her. Like many children, she did not come fully to grips with all the emotional ramifications of the missing birth link until she was well into adolescence. Her repeated expressions of hurt and disappointment, and her parents' empathetic responses, helped her develop her own capacity to compromise and to forgive. Eventually, she let her parents know that it was okay that she was not "from them," that she no longer felt sad about it. Once a child is able to forgive her adoptive parents for not giving birth to her, she is also freer to forgive her birth parents for giving her away. When Annie found that capacity for forgiveness inside her, the act of her birth parents no longer hurt as it once did.

The Telling in Trans-racial Families

Young children may seem to accept change and difference easily, but in fact, their acceptance is often based on their lack of perception. Any difference that they do observe may create fear and anxiety. For example, Cheryl Donen, mother of twenty-month-old Tommy, tells a story about the time she changed the way she wore her hair. Feeling that she was stuck in a rut, she treated herself to a visit to the beauty shop in Bergdorf Goodman for a makeover that included a stylish new short haircut. "When I walked into the house, Tommy took one look at my new haircut and began to scream. For a minute, I thought he didn't even recognize me. I don't think he forgave me for several days for turning into a 'different' mommy."

A difference in mommy is hard enough to accept. When the child gets the feeling, "I am the one who is different," it is indeed painful. That is the emotional risk faced by the child adopted by parents of a different race. It takes special sensitivity on the part of the adoptive parents to help the child cope with the issues of visible difference.

The visible differences of the adoptee of different race from the family may affect the timing of the telling. Some adoptive parents find that one of their biggest problems in choosing the right time to reveal the facts of adoption to their child is the reaction of other adults. Mrs. Jonas, for example, learned that it was impossible to stop friends from commenting on the cuteness of her Korean daughter in a way that signalled to the child that she was "different." "What a pretty little thing she is," said one of the Jonases' dinner guests about two-year-old Kim. "I just love her slanty eyes!" Kim, a bright and observant child, had perhaps already noticed the fact that her eyes were shaped differently from those of the rest of her family. Ordinarily, she would have attached no particular emotional significance to the observation, but the dinner guest's remark alerted her to the fact that the difference carried some hidden meaning.

The Jonases chose not to tell Kim about her adoption yet, because they judged that the two-year-old was not ready to understand the concept. They did what they could to protect their daughter from casual comments that might make her feel isolated and different by explaining the problem to family and close friends, and they also talked to Kim about the fact that people in a family don't always look the same. They relied on the fact that in a child as young as Kim, the feeling of family belonging, and especially the sense of oneness with the mother, acts as a powerful barrier to thoughtless or intrusive remarks that might divide a child from parents. Older children, although they are capable of understanding more about the concept of adoption and coping with their response to hurtful remarks, are also more vulnerable to the emotional wounds of such remarks.

Not all trans-racial adoptive families can arrange to live in an integrated neighborhood, as advised by adoption experts as a way of providing the adoptee with models for racial identification. But parents can easily incorporate elements into the daily life at home that symbolize the integration of their child's birth heritage with the adoptive heritage. A meal on the table that includes a dish from the cuisine of the child's heritage; music on the stereo with the melodies and rhythms of the birth background; reproductions of famous paintings by artists of kindred blood or objects made by the culture's craft workers; bedtime stories that refer to children of the birth heritage; the use of an endearment in the native language: all have a special magic in the trans-racial family. Essentially, all these activities enhance the "we-ness" of everyday life. The message communicated is, "We like it best of all that we are as we are, and we like to share our heritages with each other."

Handling the Problems

Despite careful preparation for the telling, it does not always go smoothly. The child may be less ready than the parents thought, and the parents may be less able to deal with the child's emotional response than they knew. Luckily, mistakes and problems can be dealt with in subsequent conversations about the concept. The important thing is to keep the lines of communication open.

One source of difficulty may be that something else of importance is happening in the family at the time that is appropriate for the telling. For example, the adoptive mother may become pregnant at about the time it is obvious the adoptee is showing signs of readiness to learn about adoption. Parents must consider carefully how to coordinate the telling with the arrival of a new baby in the family. Learning about adoption at that time may be a source of confusion, as it was to Sylvie Leaf.

Adopted at two months, Sylvie learned of the fact when she was about four, only days after her brother Jeffrey had been born to her adoptive parents. Visitors coming to see the new baby made thoughtless remarks, such as comments about the first birth or comparisons of family resemblances that omitted Sylvie, and thus her parents decided they could not delay the telling. At the time, the little girl showed no overt sign of difficulty. It only became apparent three years later—a long time in the life of a growing child.

In fact, the problem might never have emerged so clearly had it not been for the fact that Sylvie's grandmother, the senior Mrs. Leaf, died of a sudden heart attack the summer before Sylvie entered second grade.

The little girl and the elderly woman had been very close. Sylvie was named after her grandfather, Sylvan Leaf, who had died two months before the little girl's adoption, a link that made her special in her grandmother's eyes. And Gramma Leaf, who lived alone, had been the one to care for little Sylvie while her mother was away at work.

Sylvie's parents, absorbed in their own grief and adjustment to Mrs. Leaf's death, failed to notice that their daughter's reaction was excessive. It was her teacher, Miss Kane, who first became aware of the problem. Sylvie told her teacher about her grandmother's death within the first few days of school—how much she missed her! Miss Kane initially assumed that it was the death of a loved one that accounted for the girl's unexpectedly poor performance in second grade, so at variance with her reported abilities. As a first grader, Sylvie had been considered a bright and cooperative pupil. However, in her second year of school, she got poor grades, seemed unable to concentrate, and was so restless that she often ran around or out of the classroom without permission.

One day after school, on a day that the class had discussed the concept of God, Sylvie approached Miss Kane in the hall. The girl was having trouble buttoning her coat and needed help. Miss Kane knelt to work the big button through the stiff hole and was surprised to hear Sylvie ask, without preamble, "If God is good, why did he take my good Gramma?" Miss Kane told the child honestly that she couldn't give her an answer to that question, but she did try to offer consolation by saying she was sure Sylvie's grandmother was with God.

Sylvie evidently judged that her teacher had time to listen to her and that her feelings were being respected. Thus she continued the conversation by asking, "Am I abortion?" She did not elucidate her oddly phrased question, but only looked up expectantly at Miss Kane, hurt showing in her unhappy eyes. Miss Kane correctly guessed that this topic, whatever Sylvie meant by it, was highly significant to the little girl. Gently, she suggested that Sylvie return with her to the classroom and keep her company while she cleaned the blackboards.

As the two worked to wipe off the scribbles of the day's work, Miss Kane carefully returned to the subject Sylvie had broached. Hoping for clarification, she asked Sylvie in a neutral voice, about the word "abortion:" what did she think it meant? Sylvie answered soberly, "It means that a mother wraps up her child in a newspaper and puts it in the garbage." After a momentary pause, she demanded anxiously, "Why would a mother want abortion?"

At long last, Miss Kane had an inkling of what was wrong. Sylvie had confused the two words, "abortion" and "adoption." Worse, she seemed to be equating the idea of being adopted with the idea of being garbage— the newborn who is wrapped in yesterday's paper and thrown in the garbage pail, later to be rescued by the adoptive parents. Miss Kane reassured Sylvie that birth mothers do not put their infants in a garbage pail, no matter what. That statement was not, of course, completely true, as occasional newspaper headlines attest. Even so, Miss Kane did not think she was saying anything that would harm Sylvie's trust in her or cause a problem for Sylvie in the future.

The teacher sent the little girl home and told her to talk to her parents about the "mixed up" ideas. Her loving parents were horrified to discover how Sylvie had inadvertently knotted together the strands of bits of information with her feelings and thoughts about her life's experience. Like any child whose parents have turned over a major part of the nurturing responsibility to a grandparent, Sylvie had complex emotions about the bond between herself and her grandmother. She felt very close to the senior Mrs. Leaf; at the same time, whatever a child could make of a mother's behavior in leaving for work every morning, whatever rejection the child might find in it, Sylvie had found. And because she had learned that she lacked a biological tie to her mother before she was ready to cope with that fact's meaning, the impact of her mother's daily "abandonment" was even stronger.

Her grandmother's death felt like one more willful departure. The notion that her grandmother was "in Heaven" gave Sylvie no comfort. From a child's point of view, adults are always powerful and decisive, so she could not imagine that her grandmother had no say in going away. Sylvie reacted with anger as well as sadness, and then was frightened by the intensity of her feelings. She did not like herself any more. Her feelings were too hateful. Others must not like her either—and most especially her parents. Sylvie could not explain any of this, not even to herself, because she lacked the words and concepts to describe it. Like any child, she simply assumed that her parents could see right into her mind and discover the "badness" that was there.

Sylvie's view of herself was colored by her earlier experience of being informed that she was adopted. She may have been too immature at four to grasp the information and integrate it into her understanding of herself. Moreover, she was given the information at a time when she was having to make an adjustment to sharing her parents with her newborn baby brother Jeffrey. As she saw the family's great joy over his birth, and learned about her own adoption, she felt as if she had been given away twice: once by her birth parents to her adoptive parents, and a second time by her adoptive parents to her grandmother.

Sylvie thought that she would have been perfectly happy if only her grandmother hadn't died and left her without anyone to care about her. In reality, the hurt over what she saw as a double abandonment lay inside her, to be further darkened by the loss of her grandmother. While she was feeling so bad about herself and her unpleasant emotions, she happened to see a television show that presented the idea of adoption as an alternative to abortion. The message she received was "abortion equals adoption," and that fit with the way she was then feeling about herself.

A full understanding of what was going wrong in young Sylvie's life did not come overnight. After her parents realized her confusion and distress, the family began seeing a psychotherapist recommended by the school. With his help, Sylvie's father began to recognize that the long hours he put into his rising law career constituted a sort of abandonment of his family. More importantly for the family, Sylvie's mother reluctantly admitted to herself that she had a feeling of preference for her biological son—a fact she had never faced before. Making the admission, and facing her own feelings of guilt and inadequacy because she preferred her son, helped her to empathize with her daughter's emotions: she could understand how having bad feelings could make you feel you were bad. Meanwhile, Sylvie's therapy helped her spill out the bad feelings that had accumulated. By the end of the school year, the family was much closer, and Sylvie was feeling better about herself. On the last day of school, Sylvie kissed Miss Kane goodbye, as Mrs. Leaf said gratefully, "You did us a good deed, the whole family."

Another source of difficulty arises with the child who comes into adoption too young to use words to communicate thoughts and fantasies, yet old enough to have formed a deep attachment to a nurturing person with whom the child lived in infancy, whether foster mother or mother of birth. In this case, the major focus of the adoptive parents must be on helping their child cope with the loss of the earlier relationship and learning to trust them. The explanation of the adoptive relationship must be handled carefully to meet these needs.

Ellen Ronson recalls how unequal she felt to fulfilling all that she perceived her daughter needed from the telling. Katherine was about two years old when Ellen and Jake Ronson adopted her. She had spent those first two years with a foster mother to whom she had a deep attachment. When the Ronsons first met her at the foster mother's home, they had spoken to the two-year-old the words that would later be meaningful, such as "foster mother," "birth mother," and "adopt." Too young to understand any of the concepts, Katherine simply smiled and indicated she wanted to play. The relationship between the Ronsons and Katherine developed steadily, and soon the day came when they picked her up one final time to take her to her new home. Katherine cried long and sadly, which the Ronsons considered a hopeful sign. It is better for a child to feel the pain of a separation than to deny it, because denied pain usually remains hidden in the far reaches of the mind, ready to cause problems at some later date.

Katherine seemed to adapt to her new situation well, experiencing no interruption in her development. In the early days of her adoption, she frequently expressed her longing for "Nannie", as she called her foster mother, and Ellen and Jake were always there to comfort her. As time passed, she mentioned Nannie less and less often. Her parents, mindful of the fact that it is best to allow the child to lead the way in introducing a painful subject, did not raise the topic of Nannie.

One day, about two years after Katherine's adoption, the four-year-old was sitting at the kitchen table with her mother after breakfast. Unexpectedly, she burst out, "I want Nannie!"

Ellen, surprised to hear the subject reintroduced, answered supportively. "I know you want her, darling, but you live with us now. You are our adopted daughter." To Ellen's even greater surprise, Katherine asked, "What is 'adopted'?" Apparently, the little girl had "forgotten" all that Ellen and Jake had told her about adoption. Gently, Ellen reiterated, "You know, adopted means you are going to live with Daddy and me forever, until you are all grown up. We all belong together now. You were born of birth parents who loved you but could not take care of you—."

Katherine interrupted, "That was Nannie?"

"No," answered Ellen. "Nannie was your foster mother. She loved you, too."

Katherine was on the edge of tears. "You mean . . . I have three mommies?"

Ellen took a deep breath. Patiently, she repeated the information she and her husband had given their daughter many times: The "Nannie" whom Katherine remembered with love was her foster mother, who had loved her and taken care of her until she was adopted. Another woman, her birth mother, had given birth to her and also loved her but couldn't take care of her. Ellen was the mommy who loved her and with whom she would stay "forever" until she was grown up.

Inwardly, Ellen worried that what she was saying left her daughter emotionally unsatisfied and intellectually confused. It was upsetting to realize that Katherine still felt the loss of Nannie so keenly. How could she help her daughter, she wondered.

Ellen was already doing everything for Katherine that could be done, by letting the little girl express her feelings and helping her accept them. It is not easy for a four-year-old to understand having three mommies, but that was the reality of Katherine's life. She was doing her best to cope with the confusing information about herself and her anxiety about what that information meant. Her forgetfulness about her birth mother might have been the consequence of not wanting to know about her in the first place. Having even two mommies can be distressing to a child Katherine's age, and having three is just too difficult to accept quickly or readily.

At four, Katherine was much too young to understand the concepts she had to confront, including not only adoption but also the institution of foster care as distinct from that of adoption. The fact that adoption would improve her long-term situation was no comfort to her for losing the foster mother she remembered with such attachment, and at that age, she might gladly have traded in her adoptive parents for a chance to return to Nannie.

Yet Katherine was making an excellent adjustment as an adopted child. The explanations her mother gave her of the concepts of adoption and foster care could not be particularly relevant at that early period of her life, but she did understand the intent behind them. Like most children, Katherine was exquisitely aware of her parents' intentions, and she recognized the love and sensitivity to her needs that lay behind the confusing answers Ellen could give her. That awareness, coupled with the freedom she felt to express herself, eventually made her "bad" feelings go away. It healed the hurt.

Another kind of problem may arise with children who learn about their adoption before they fully understand the birth process. For example, Larry, who had lived with his adoptive parents almost since birth, was informed of his adoption a few weeks before his third birthday. He reacted at first with disbelief. His father (a physician) and mother were amused to hear Larry soon afterward speaking of himself as "doctor boy." His mother later acknowledged that his confusion of the word "doctor" and "adopted" should have alerted them to the fact that something was amiss, but at the time, they interpreted it as "adorable" and a sign of his attachment to and identification with his doctor father.

Two years later, Larry's parents learned from his kindergarten teacher that he was quite comfortable in telling the class he was adopted—no problems any more in confusing the word. The teacher also reported that their bright little boy had an odd theory about his birth, one he had not mentioned at home. Larry had told his teacher that he was born, not of any human being, but of something inanimate: a box on the office shelf of the agency that had arranged his adoption. There were two types of children, he had explained carefully, those born of human mothers and those born of boxes at the adoption agency. Larry had also told friends at school about his wondrous birth, although he showed no signs of considering it remarkable.

His parents remembered the day they had taken Larry with them to the adoption agency, when they were applying to adopt a younger child. Apparently, he had seen file boxes on the office shelves, and arrived at his own conclusions about what they contained. But his confusion was rooted in the fact that, when Larry learned of his adoption, he was too young to take in full details of the birth process, including the sexual act, conception and gestation. Many children develop theories of birth that eliminate the sexual act, and parents may mistakenly cooperate with such fantasies. Stories about the stork, for example, or babies found under a cabbage, were acceptable to generations of families. For an adoptee, however, understanding of the birth process is necessary to an understanding of the concept of birth parents and adoption. While Larry was perhaps just as pleased to think he didn't come out of his mother's tummy, he was unable to imagine a real birth mother. Lack of information about her—not even a snapshot— increased her unreality and thus the unreality of his birth. It took some time, and many gentle repetitions of the facts about his birth by his parents, for Larry to understand that his birth was just like that of every other child . . . in other words, that he was fully human.

Some Special Ways to Help

Adoptive parents who are able to communicate with the birth mother before the adoption might ask her to write the child a letter, to be opened on a certain date, such as the child's eighteenth birthday. Ideally, the letter should explain the mother's decision in a positive way: "I wanted a better life for you, and a family for you that I could not give." Such a statement is both true and meaningful to an adoptee. It comforts and consoles, because the good intention of the birth mother—and every birth mother who arranges to have her child adopted intends well—illuminates the words, even years after the event. The letter should also include physical details: her height and coloring, and that of the father (and perhaps a snapshot of both of them); information about the grandparents, such as vocation and ethnic origin, and about other relatives. Medical information and genetic background will be helpful for the adoptee later in life.

Although reading the letter will take place at a later date, the mere existence of a communication from the birth mother will help comfort the adoptee. Adopted children often feel a deep sense of loss because nothing—or almost nothing—is known about what they were like before they came to their adoptive home. That loss can be mitigated by a letter from the birth mother. A letter from a foster mother may serve the same purpose for the child who is adopted months or years after birth.

Whether or not it has been possible to secure a letter from the birth mother or foster mother, adoptive parents should make their own collection of special memories and details about the child from the moment of entering the family. Parents who started a memory book when their child first came to them find it a useful tool during the telling, and throughout the coming years as the subject is discussed again and again. Together, the family can look at the snapshots taken the first day. They look at the names of other people who figured in the adoption process, such as the judge, lawyer, doctor, or social worker. They retell the details of important events of the child's first weeks and month in the family. The memory book is part of the larger story of the adoptive family and how it grows.

The concrete details preserved in a letter or a memory book are especially meaningful to an adoptee, because in some measure they substitute for the lost connection to the family of one's blood. They give the child the sense of being grounded in time and place that the rest of society takes for granted but adoptees often speak of missing.

Rhoda and Burt Hirsch realized the importance of giving their adopted daughter a sense of her roots after they made their own first visit to Germany one summer, while nine-year-old Alix was away at summer camp. Themselves the children of Jewish families that had managed to escape Germany on the eve of World War II, the Hirsches felt that the trip helped them find a new sense of "legacy" and pride in the world of their parents and grandparents, and to "forgive" the present German nation for the events of the Holocaust.

On their return, Rhoda and Burt realized that their previous feelings of having had the past torn away from them by the Holocaust were similar to the feelings Alix must have about her own lost past. Like the majority of adoptees, Alix had no information about her birth family, no hint of ethnic background, no idea where her birth parents had been born, no suggestion of a part of the country with which the family of her blood was identified. She had no description of her birth parents or other relatives, no keepsake such as a toy or picture. The only piece of concrete information available was the name of the hospital in New York City where she had been born.

Alix, who had made a good adjustment to adoption, did not mention any feelings of loss in regard to her past. She was energetically involved with her family and friends. She seemed happy at school and in her activities in the children's program of the Temple to which the Hirsches belonged. Yet she responded with great happiness when her parents proposed a trip the following summer to visit the scene of her birth.

The pilgrimage the Hirsch family made the summer Alix was ten, driving from their home in California three thousand miles across the country, became one of Alix's happiest memories. The family stayed at a motel near the hospital, with a rooftop pool in which Alix paddled every morning. They did some sightseeing in the city, and every day, they visited the hospital where Alix was born. It was a huge institution on the banks of the Hudson River, and Burt, Rhoda, and Alix wandered around the entire complex. They took many snapshots, showing them in various locations: on the steps in front of the massive front doors, strolling the tree-lined garden walk used by student nurses, eating in the cafeteria, walking the corridors of the obstetrics wing, and looking out windows at the view of the broad river passing by.

Alix pasted those snapshots in an album when she got back home, and she always remembered the good feelings of that time. Although the trip could not change the reality that she had been given away by her birth parents, it symbolized the understanding of her adoptive parents that made it, after all, "okay." They had given her a life. She liked it as it was, and would not change it for any other.

4 Imagination and Reality

While the adoptee has to grow and mature just as other children do, an adoptive child's imagination almost inevitably incorporates certain themes that make the task of understanding reality, an essential aspect of adulthood, more difficult. A characteristic challenge is differentiating the real (adoptive) parents from the unknown but imagined birth parents—which is like the task of differentiating the child's real dual identity (birth and adoptive) from an imagined one. Fortunately, adopted children, like others, do send out messages about what is on their minds, as they try to make sense of their world of experience and get comfort and pleasure for themselves. When parents understand the messages, they can use the power of family communication to help.

The story of three-year-old Jimmy illustrates how an adopted child creates an imaginary picture of his unknown birth mother, which is based on his real-life adoptive mother. It also suggests how parents can respond to help their child keep a positive view and learn about reality at the same time. Allan and Martha had adopted Jimmy when he was eleven weeks old. The full-term baby had been born healthy and strong. A foster mother cared for him from the time of his birth, but his adoption came before he was old enough to experience the strength of attachment to her that is signalled by stranger anxiety. Therefore his first deep feelings were for Martha. Jimmy had the happy exuberance of a toddler totally confident of his parents' love and of his own abilities. He interpreted even ambiguous events as good. A cup of milk was half full, not half empty, as far as he was concerned. He expected his future to be as satisfying as his past. He believed in his own essential goodness, and belief in himself went hand in hand with his belief in his parents.

Jimmy gradually became aware that he was adopted, although he probably did not grasp the full meaning of the concept. For no particular reason that his parents could recall, he became especially interested in the idea that he had a birth mother, another mother, and was trying to make sense of the concept. Martha thought that the boy did not seem particularly concerned about the thought that he had been given away, but rather focused on the notion that his birth mother was real, and that he had a real connection to her.

One evening, Jimmy was using all of a little boy's tactics to delay his bedtime. For any child, going to bed means a break in the feeling of ordinary connectedness to the family. When there is a reason for the sense of the break to be heightened, such as even the temporary absence of a parent, or a move to a new room, it can be felt as a kind of isolation that frightens. That is the reason some children fear the dark. In the mind of the young adoptee, the concept of birth parents represents an additional break in the sense of belonging to the family. As a baby, Jimmy had had the blissful experience of being held by his mother that is vital for all children, had incorporated it into his emotional fiber, and he was not afraid of the dark. But probably he did want to avoid the sense of aloneness that children often experience as they are falling asleep. So he was plying Martha with questions that pertained to his birth and his birth mother's existence. Martha was careful to respond unhurriedly, for she knew that a leisurely discussion is supportive of a child's curiosity.

"What kind of room was I born in?" asked Jimmy.

"I believe you were born in a hospital room, like other children. Yes, I believe so," answered Martha.

Wriggling out of his cotton polo shirt, Jimmy noticed the apple tree outside the bedroom window. He demanded, "Did my other mother have a tree outside her window?" Martha replied, "Yes, she probably did have a tree outside her window." As Martha crossed the room to hang his shirt on the closet door hook, Jimmy asked, "Did she have a closet in her room too?" "I think she must have had a closet," answered Martha patiently. "Did she sleep in a bed like mine?" her son continued, as Martha pulled down his spread. "Yes," responded Martha, "she probably did."

"Mommy, Mommy," said Jimmy as Martha placed his battered teddy bear at the foot of the bed, "did she give me a toy? If she did, oh boy, I want it!" Martha answered honestly that she did not know about a toy but that she would try to find out for him. That satisfied Jimmy, and he became absorbed in the bedtime story Martha began to read.

In this conversation, Jimmy called for information that is especially important to an adopted child. He wanted to know that he was born in the same manner as all other children, and that his birth mother was a regular person, like himself and his adoptive parents. (Many adopted children have secret fantasies that they must have come from outer space, perhaps like Superman, and that their birth parents were not human beings.) Jimmy, satisfied by Martha's consistent and positive answers that hypothesized and referred to general situations, then turned to his final question: Could he perceive his birth mother as a human being with whom he might have a real, if limited, child-parent tie?

After making his claim to the toy that represented the link, Jimmy confidently relinquished his questioning of Martha about his birth mother. His expectation that Martha would find the toy reflected his feeling about her, not about his unknown birth mother. He assumed that all parents are by nature giving. As a receiver of gifts from his parents—gifts of the heart as well as of the tangible variety—he had had no other experience. Interpreted in the language of adults, his view might be summarized this way: *I have belonged to my mother since the time beyond memory and she has belonged to me. She understands me. She anticipates and fills my needs. She is the embodiment of my ideal. Therefore, I have no doubt that she can now do as I wish, find a way to establish a connection between me and that other woman that they have told me about. Although I do not know and have not known the other woman, I imagine that she is good, too, and could serve as another model for my ideal.*

As the concept of his adoption was becoming more meaningful, Jimmy could no longer continue to take his relationship to his mother completely for granted. Adoption interfered and perhaps created a doubt. Jimmy restored his equilibrium by using the power of his imagination. He created a comforting image of his birth mother that resembled—who else?—his beloved Martha.

The Power of Fantasy

Many children use their imagination the way Jimmy did, once they are aware that they are adopted. His wished-for toy was a concrete symbol that helped make a phantom-like birth mother real. Children of his age have a difficult time comprehending abstractions: anything that cannot be seen, heard, tasted, touched, smelled, or represented in a picture or story. With his questions and imagined toy, Jimmy attempted to create a concrete picture of a giving woman to heal himself of his feelings of loss—both the temporary one, the everyday world that slips away as sleep comes, and the permanent one that came from the understanding that he was not physically born of Allan and Martha. Adoptive parents who respond warmly, as Jimmy's did, to their child's curiosity about birth parents set up the possibility for further adoptive communication later on, as the child's maturing process causes a continual widening of interests and questions. It helps when they understand that their child's interest in the birth mother is a tribute to them and not a criticism.

In the mind of a three-year-old like Jimmy, thinking and feeling are almost the same. Children that age have not yet learned to differentiate between feelings and logical thoughts. The younger the child is, the more likely he or she is to think with the feelings. For example, when a young child's tummy hurts, the world becomes a bad place. And to think with feelings is to create a fantasy, as Jimmy did, through which he attempted to solve a problem that his life as an adopted child presented him. His imagination was the handmaiden of his needs, born of his wish to heal himself of a feeling of disconnectedness, and at the same time to comprehend the unknown. Inexperienced as his young imagination was, Jimmy's ability to question, "How can I get what I need and want?" and his competence in selecting models from the real objects and relationships of his world, powered its dynamics.

Jimmy's interest in his birth mother can be compared to that of Mark. His view was as positive as Jimmy's, but his fantasies took a different form, as befitted an older child. Mark was five years old when he surprised his adoptive mother, Violet, as she was drying him off after his bath one evening. Out of the blue, he casually remarked that he would like to meet his birth mother. "What would you like to do?" asked Violet, a little too sharply. He explained, "I'd like to be grown up so I could take her out to dinner." Violet, who was beginning to understand what her son was trying to communicate, responded sympathetically, "I guess that would be lots of fun." Her elliptical statement meant, "I hypothesize that you believe that as your birth mother's benefactor, you would have lots of fun." It mirrored in positive fashion Mark's wish, and at the same time, by its hypothetical emphasis, injected a note of reality. A hypothetical statement refers to possibility, not actuality. Mark seemed satisfied with his mother's answer. He did not pursue the topic but turned instead to an account of how he won a game of cards he had played with his father, Tony, earlier that evening.

Mark expressed his curiosity and warm interest in birth family matters again, some months later. He had recently entered the first grade and was enjoying himself hugely. The intellectual stimulation and the new friendships could not have been more satisfying. That particular evening, he was dawdling over his dinner. The others had almost finished, while his plate was still full. His big brother Kevin (a biological child of Tony and Violet) noticed. "What's on *your* mind?" he asked. Mark answered that he was thinking about his other mother. Violet and Tony fell silent, while Kevin carried on the conversation. "Tell me," he demanded.

Mark mused aloud. "What was she like? What was her mommy and daddy like? I'm thinking about it in chapters. Chapter 1 is her. That's all I did so far." Mark's reference to chapters was based on his teacher's recent mention of a book the class would soon be reading, the first they'd had that was divided into chapters. Mark's imagined "book of the birth family" was a more abstract device than Jimmy's toy, but it was an equivalent connection to his birth family. And also like Jimmy, he drew on his real life experience to create his fantasy. His was an adaptation of his teacher's gift to him (as he perceived her discussion of the forthcoming book) as appropriate at six years of age as Jimmy's use of parental gifts had been at an earlier age.

Tony finally entered the conversation. "Right you are, son. Everyone should have a special chapter in your book. Let's talk about it some more after dinner. Right now, I'd like to see you dig into those mashed potatoes and clean your plate."

In this manner, Tony demonstrated to Mark that his interests were worthwhile, as well as providing him with an object lesson in the skill of communicating—by his focus on the importance of choosing when to talk about a particular subject, in a time of its own rather than at dinnertime. While all children who possess the skills to speak of important things are fortunate, for adopted Mark it would be a necessity, critical to his being able to achieve a full understanding of the complex situation that was his.

The family discussion, after they'd finished eating dessert but were still at the dining table, was brief. Mark did not say anything more, but waited expectantly. It seemed clear that he wanted to hear from the others. After his mother and brother expressed their appreciation and support of Mark's notion, his father spoke again. He suggested that Mark might be able to fill in a "book of the birth family" after he was grown up. The boy asked why he had to be grown up, and Tony explained that they would go together to look for the information, after his eighteenth birthday. Mark, used to hearing that the future held options for him that he was presently too young to exercise, found Tony's statement quite acceptable. "I hope you don't mind waiting to fill in your book, son," added Tony, in a slightly apologetic tone. Mark nodded cheerfully. "It's okay, Dad. I can wait." The family discussion was at an end.

Tony wisely chose not to go into the social issues and organizational policies regarding disclosures of birth family identity. Mark did not seem interested in this topic, and probably was not ready to pursue his questions to that extreme. His parents were also aware that the wished-for information might never materialize, no matter how thorough a search the family made later. But they did not want to discourage Mark's present expectations. If trying to carry out his wish did eventually come to a dead end, his family would be sharing the disappointment with him. Being emotionally together in the searching experience with one's adoptive family is a powerful comfort for a youngster, one that helps to soften a final letdown, if that should be the result.

Fantasies of the Good Mother and the Bad Mother

In the world of childhood fantasy, nothing remains as it is in reality. The figures are larger than life, blown up to overpowering size, idealized or denigrated. Yet no matter how far and wide a child's imagination ranges, it is always based in the reality of the past. Adult figures are modeled after a child's real-life parents; other important figures are modeled after the child's own self—the little prince or princess, the lost orphan, naughty Peter. Imagination works to transfigure reality.

The first act of a child's imagination is the formation of a special illusion: that one's mother and oneself are part of a singular whole, a unit that has no meaningful division. An infant under six months of age is not aware that there are boundaries to things, finite beginnings and endings. For a time, we all know no difference between "outside" and "inside," and have no inkling of a division between the actual environment and the self who perceives it. But at a certain point in the child's maturation process, everything changes. The infant begins to see a particular mother as the unique person that she is. There is a sense of anxiety and loss when she is not present. The breakup of the child's illusion of oneness with the mother begins.

Yet the memory of the happiness of being held in mother's arms and the illusion of feeling at one with her remains throughout life, and surfaces from time to time in other forms. One derivation that all children know is the *Fantasy of the Good Mother*. The child uses it to cope with the discomfort that comes in the wake of the dawning knowledge of being a separate, helpless being.

Thirteen-month-old Ronny, who was born in Korea and brought to the United States at eight weeks, was able to wait quietly alone, even when he felt hungry and wet, because he had a warm mental image of Marie, his adoptive mother. The image was glorified as SHE WHO IS ALWAYS THERE WHEN I NEED HER. The next best thing to Marie herself, the child's idealization was not too far from the truth. Ronny's mother would have liked always to be there, and she did try her best. Yet she recognized that she probably could never exactly live up to his wishes. From time to time, when her actions did not exactly fit the comforting ideal that her son had been expecting—her expression was a trifle harried, her touch abrupt—she knew that she would hear from him in anger and distress.

At such times, Ronny's fantasy of Marie as the Good Mother would have gone sour and turned into its opposite, the *Fantasy of the Bad Mother:* SHE WHO IS NOT CARING OF MY EVERY WISH. Intuitively, Marie understood she would then have to re-establish her child's sense of the rightness of his world, the trust that she and the Good Mother of his fantasies were one and the same. Her soothing gestures and kisses would mean in reality, "I am sorry, I did not neglect you on purpose. Look, now I am making it all better." Shortly, all would be well again in the world of the nursery. Ronny's disappointment would evaporate as his roseate expectations were restored.

Of course, Ronny's mother had not stopped loving him because she tried to introduce a new food he didn't like. But Ronny attributed to his mother the unpleasant taste in his mouth, as he made clear by his wail and his angry stare into her eyes. Ronny interpreted the unwelcome new taste of the green stuff in the spoon not as the unfamiliar flavor of peas, but as a literal piece of his mother. What she spooned into his rejecting mouth was not a vegetable, it was herself. If it tasted bad, then she must be the Bad Mother.

Shifting fantasies about the Good Mother and the Bad Mother are characteristic of all children. However, because an adopted child's life is always more complicated (once the child is aware of the adoption or of a change in the beloved nurturing person) certain of the child's fantasies are more complicated and need more understanding. The child whose experiences have already been unhappy—who has suffered the loss of a loved caregiver, or has endured physical pain or emotional neglect—will especially be more absorbed in negative fantasies. That is true even of young babies. Though they are not yet able to think, theirs is a wordless power of the imagination.

The Distortion of Memory through Fantasy

All children who must relinquish their first love (a loving birth mother or foster mother) risk a particular problem of the fantasy life: that first attachment, which was very good in reality, can turn bad in memory. To adopted Leanna, that is what actually happened.

Before her adoption, Leanna had matured to the stage where she expected to have the sense of perfect union she felt with her beloved foster mother, "Mammy", continue unbroken forever. (The infant, who has not yet achieved a sense of time, feels even a single moment as forever.) Leanna was a thriving eighteen-month-old toddler when she went to live with Shirley and Joel, her adoptive parents. Before leaving her foster home, she had been carefully prepared for the change. But there was no way that the toddler could be prepared for the difficult reality of losing her relationship with the one person she loved above all others, her foster mother. Leanna was too young to grasp the idea that change would mean loss.

Not long after Leanna came to her new family, she became seriously constipated. Constipation is a common symptom in an infant who has deep feelings of loss. It represents an infant's way, inappropriate though it may be, of trying to hold on to the past. With her pediatrician's advice, Shirley altered Leanna's diet, and the condition righted itself. Then a different symptom of Leanna's feelings of loss arose. It was more mysterious and did not yield so quickly. Leanna began to have nightmares. On first analysis, their content seemed incomprehensible. The little girl dreamed that her foster mother came to her, no longer loving nor the dream image of the benign Good Mother, but a frightening image of an evil witch. Mammy came to kidnap Leanna away from Shirley and Joel.

The first time she had this nightmare, little Leanna screamed out in her sleep. "No! No! Mammy is going to come back and get me!" Shirley ran into the child's room and took her up in her arms. Gently, she reassured

Leanna. "No, sweetie," she said. "You will stay with us forever. Mammy loved you but she could not keep you and she is not coming to get you." Shirley repeated the phrase, "You'll stay with us forever," until Leanna fell asleep.

The little girl continued to dream repetitively of being taken away from her new home by a witch-like Mammy for another three months. The final screaming episode occurred very early one winter morning. Leanna awakened the household with her loud sobs, screaming that "the animals" were coming to get her. Animals in this context symbolize the Bad Mother of fantasy. But as soon as her adoptive mother picked her up, Leanna stopped crying and relaxed. Seeing her daughter's readiness to take comfort, Shirley hoped she would be able to get right back to her own interrupted sleep. First, though, she would croon a lullaby she had made up on one of the earlier occasions when Leanna had been upset by a nightmare. The song called for Leanna to participate, and it had a reassuring message for her. It went like this:

> **SHIRLEY** (in a sing-song voice): Do you know why I am staying here with you?

> **LEANNA:** Because you love me!

> **SHIRLEY:** Yes!

> **LEANNA:** Because you are never going to leave me!

> **SHIRLEY:** Right!

> **LEANNA:** Because I'm going to stay with you forever.

SHIRLEY: *Yes!*

After several repetitions, Shirley ended the song this way:

SHIRLEY: *But I'd like to go to bed—right now.*

LEANNA: *Yes!*

Leanna then allowed Shirley to turn off the light and leave. It was the last time she woke with those nightmares. The little girl had resolved her fantasy of the Bad Mother, at least for the time being.

Leanna's distress at the enormous change that had recently taken place in her life was first expressed through her constipation. But she was still left with her intense anger at her foster mother for "going bye-bye forever," her blame of Mammy for their separation and her feeling that Mammy no longer cared for her. Such feelings are understandable in her situation as an adoptee. (Children who lose a parent through death often react this way too.) Yet the particular form in which her feelings were expressed seemed initially confusing, as her anger and fear worked on her imagination to turn Mammy from a Good Mother into a Bad Mother. The little girl's balance was restored by her adoptive mother's loving constancy, her calm reassurance, her absolute certainty of Mammy's goodness and love for Leanna.

Leanna's fears and anger surfaced again after she began to attend nursery school. That was not surprising. A child needs repeated and varying experiences of coping in order to develop the ability to handle so serious a problem as the loss of the first beloved and to be able to face a situation that reminds her of the past without anxiety. One day Shirley had picked her daughter up after school and Leanna, then four years old, solemnly stated, "I didn't have a good day today." She explained that her class had a substitute teacher, whom she didn't like. The following morning, Leanna wanted to stay at home, but she admitted she was not ill. Shirley questioned her further about the previous day and learned that Leanna thought the substitute teacher looked like the social worker who had taken her away from Mammy more than two years earlier. Shirley herself did not remember what the social worker looked like, but she answered reassuringly, "She may look a lot like the lady, but she is NOT the lady. Anyway, nobody is going to take you away from us." Leanna was satisfied and willingly returned to nursery school.

A few months later, her problem emerged again. Leanna had overheard the mother of one of her friends at school angrily explain to the teacher, "Peter is a bad boy and hasn't changed since coming here. I can't cope with him at home. He must go to a strict boarding institution." She added that she was immediately removing Peter from the nursery school. Afterward, Leanna watched her teacher closely, and saw her talking about Peter to another teacher. Leanna wrongly interpreted her teacher's conversation as meaning that she was in league with the little boy's mother and that she too wanted to "get rid" of him.

After Peter was taken out of her nursery school, Leanna became disobedient and destructive. In fact, she behaved much as Peter had, painting on the walls and breaking many toys. Her fantasy of the Bad Mother had been aroused, and she responded to it by behaving in her real-life situation as "bad," too, like her friend. Fortunately, Leanna was able to talk with her parents about what was happening, and they in turn discussed it with her teacher. Thereafter, whenever the teacher noticed Leanna acting disruptively or destructively, she reassured the girl, saying, "What happened to Peter will not happen to you." One day during this period, Leanna was able to voice her fears directly to her mother, asking Shirley, "What about you, Mom, will you send me away for being naughty?" Shirley responded with reassurance (and relief that Leanna had been able to express in words what was bothering her). "You are with us forever, no matter what," she answered warmly. Leanna's behavior soon returned to normal. Clearly, her imagination had been quieted.

It was several more years before Leanna was finally able to stop reacting to separations as if they were intended to be punishments. By the time she was ready to leave grade school, however, she appeared unusually secure in her social relationships, as her teachers routinely noted on her report cards. Perhaps that was because she had had those earlier opportunities to work through her distress with adults who understood what she was communicating with them. Children who can work through their serious problems in their early years often seem, when they are older, to be stronger in their emotional life than are their contemporaries who had no such problems in the first place.

The Fantasy of a Blood Tie to Adoptive Parents

Many adopted children have the fantasy that they have always been part of their adoptive family; in other words, they imagine that their identity is NOT adoptive. That is true of children who were adopted at an age when they might have retained a memory of earlier experiences outside the adoptive family, and also true of children who have no organized memory of the period before they entered the adoptive family but have heard about it from their parents. The fantasy may serve to help some children cope with the disconcerting knowledge that a blood tie to their parents is missing. It may be the case that their belief in the importance of the blood tie is in itself illusory. It is known, after all, that the strongest parent-child link comes from the shared daily experiences of nurturing and mutual caring. Nevertheless, the idea of the importance of blood lineage has a powerful, mysterious hold on society at large. The adoptee is no different. However, if an adopted child is not pressured about the issue, the child will let go of the denial of reality when the right time comes in the maturing process. It is best that adoptive parents neither support nor interfere with the child's fantasy of a blood tie to the family.

On the other hand, adoptive parents do need to support the reality of the family status. An occasional acknowledgement, appropriately handled, will not be perceived as a threat by the youngster. Some families reinforce the reality of their adoptive status by celebrating the date of their child's coming into the family, making that date a kind of second birthday for the adoptee. But a child may not be comfortable with the practice of two birthdays each year, and the ritual may make them feel unnecessarily singled out. If adoption is a matter of the entire family, why should one individual alone be the focus of the celebration? A preferable option

might be that the whole family joins in an annual celebration of their adoptive status. They might attend a
party given by an organization of adoptive families, or
they might create their own family tradition of celebration, with an annual family outing or a backyard barbecue for friends and family.

Scott and Joanna Steinert, the adoptive parents of
Nicky, found their own solution to helping their son
reconcile the fantasy of a blood tie with the reality of
adoptive family status. Nicky had lived with a foster
mother from his fourth day of life to his fourteenth
month, when the Steinerts adopted him. They considered his foster mother a wonderful person, to whom they
were deeply grateful for her loving and superb care of
Nicky in the early months of his life. They thought of her
with affection, and wanted to find a way to include her
in Nicky's life. But the policy of the agency through
which Nicky's adoption was arranged was against main-
taining a longterm tie with her; the agency viewed it as
harmful to the adoptee's emotional development, painful
for the adoptive parents, and uncomfortable for the foster family. Desirous of finding a good compromise,
Joanna talked the situation over with her pediatrician,
an elderly man with a lifetime of experience behind his
words of wisdom. He suggested it was natural to think of
the boy's foster mother as a sort of relative. "If Nicky
had been cared for by a grandmother or great aunt who
lived far away, you would not pretend that she ceased to
exist because the separation had pain in it," he commented. Joanna also thought that when Nicky was older,
perhaps in his teens, the experience of meeting his foster
mother again might seem a gift. Youngsters who feel
secure in their adoptive families like to hear first-hand

about their earliest times, and to know the person who loved and cared for them then.

Encouraged in their decision to keep in touch with Nicky's foster mother, Joanna and Scott remembered to speak of her at special times, such as Nicky's birthday. They exchanged Christmas cards with her every year, and when Nicky was old enough, he added his own signature to the card. They planned that she would attend his Bar Mitzvah, perhaps even spend the weekend in their home. "To our way of looking at it," said Joanna, "she is a well-loved, if geographically distant, member of the family. She will always be important to us."

Even before Joanna and Scott had taken Nicky from his foster mother's home, they felt a wish to preserve for him his good experience of life with her. As they were saying goodbye at the door of the foster family's home for the last time, Joanna had handed the baby over to Scott and run impulsively back to Nicky's room, looking for something she could take along that would uniquely represent his early months with his foster family. She found only a little green tractor that she and Scott had brought Nicky on their first visit; he had not liked it and never played with it. Now it would have to do. With his foster mother's permission, Joanna stuffed the toy down into her tote bag, overflowing with bottles, diapers, and snacks.

"I thought he could have it for a keepsake," she explained to her husband as he started the car to take Nicky home. "He isn't going to need a keepsake of us," Scott noted. Joanna responded, "I know it isn't logical . . . Maybe he can just enjoy playing with it."

Nicky never did play with the tractor, but it became an important object in his room, placed on the table beside his bed. Even after his crib was exchanged for a bed, and the delicate nursery colors replaced by bright primary hues, it remained.

Nicky had no more than the ordinary difficulties in adjusting to the change in his life. His parents were somewhat puzzled that he never asked for his foster mother, and that he had accepted her loss so quietly. The fact that he seemed to have a stronger bond to Scott than to Joanna may have been an indication that even though he did not apparently remember his foster mother, he remembered the emotions of losing her. It was easier for him to trust the permanence of a father than a mother.

Even with all his parents' support of the reality of the family's adoptive status, Nicky at the age of eight had not yet let go of his denial. His wish was to be the biological child of his adoptive parents. He was still young enough to believe that a good wish could come true—and if a good wish could come true, it followed that it could be believed as truth. At the same time, like other children of his age, he was fully aware of the difference between his wishes and reality, and in this he was also supported by his parents, who had never themselves needed to deny his adoptive status.

One day, Nicky's third-grade teacher gave the class an assignment: write a composition about your favorite toy. This is what Nicky wrote.

My Favorite Toy

My favorite toy is a little green tractor. It
moves by itself. I have had it since I was born.
My Mom and Dad bought it when I was born.
Every night when I went to sleep, I played with

it. I like the noise the wheels make when they
turn. I've liked it for years.

Nicky's teacher gave his composition an A, and he
proudly showed it to his parents. They recognized their
gift of long ago. Later they asked each other, "What does
it mean?" "He never played with that truck when he was
little," said Scott. Joanna concurred. "He told me he
didn't want it and I should throw it out! If I had not been
such a sentimentalist, it would have gone long, long
ago."

It seemed that Nicky had authored a benign fantasy.
Like any good storyteller, he implied more than he had
actually said: belief in the goodness of his parents, belief
in himself. His toy seemed to be a live thing, something
that could move under its own power: himself. It was
"the toy who is me" and "the toy who is of them."
Nicky's composition made his parents feel proud, too.
They understood that he had symbolized the wholeness
of his life through his toy. His factual inaccuracy this
time was probably poetic license, not an adoptee's error.

Joanna and Scott put Nicky's story away in a safe
place. He would have it when he was grown.

5 The Resilient Child

All parents want their child to be resilient in the face of the inevitable ups and downs of existence. The person who can bounce back emotionally has a better life, both as a child and also later as an adult. Researchers of human behavior have lately turned their attention to the careful observation of what makes a child resilient. Their studies suggest that a paramount requirement is a happy and healthy babyhood.

A Healthy Babyhood

Adoptive parents yearn to give the best of everything to their child, but they are also aware that a healthy babyhood is not necessarily guaranteed for an adoptee. Even parents fortunate enough to arrange to adopt at birth know that their anticipated little one's later adjustment could be subject to the consequences of pre-natal complications, poor care during pregnancy, and/or birth trauma. So adoptive parents often become involved in assisting the birth mother with the financial demands of good care during pregnancy and the best medical attention at the time of birth.

Parents who adopt an older child may face a number of physical problems that arise from their child's early life. A child who started life in a birth family, for example, is likely to have gone through a period of inadequate care, which is often the stimulus that leads to the decision that adoption is the best resolution for the infant. Also, the child's emotional reaction to the change of environment itself may be expressed in health-related ways, such as increased crying, difficulties in feeding or sleeping, and digestive upsets. If the infant has already become psychologically attuned to a care-giver, the reaction to that person's loss may be one of active grief, with noticeable physical consequences. The child's dismay is also observed in behavioral ways: searching with the eyes and body for the one who is missing, or actions that are listless and withdrawing, such as refusing to play, to smile, even to eat.

Infants from foreign countries may also be at risk for certain medical problems that are unusual in the United States, such as intestinal parasites and scabies. They may be vulnerable, too, to certain childhood diseases, such as measles or diphtheria, because they did not receive the immunizing shots that are standard in this country. A good pediatrician can be the adoptive family's best advisor in regard to providing the healthiest babyhood possible, especially if the infant's medical history is unknown or inadequate, or if the child was born under adverse medical conditions.

A Happy Babyhood

Beyond getting good advice about medical care, the adoptive parents must also always be ready to absorb and diffuse the upset occasioned by the child's environmental change and the loss of the earlier love attachment. Luckily, parents can communicate to their babies the devotion that heals without words, just through their actions. "I love having Derek," said accountant Annette Benedict, home on a six-month leave to care for the son who arrived from Korea the month before. As an afterthought she added, "But I never realized how much laundry you have to do for an infant—I do at least one load every day!" She was sighing and laughing all in the same breath, but her expression was unmistakably one of happiness and pride in fulfilling her role as a mother.

Adoptive parents communicate their devotion to the newly arrived baby through endless caring and comforting. And although the baby cannot respond to parental love in words, the fact that the message is received is demonstrated in the child's vibrant good health. The details of each story are unique, but the nurturing love and commitment by the adoptive parents are universal.

Learning the Skills of Resilience

Researchers, among them E. James Anthony (Anthony and Cohler, 1987) have found that the ability to adapt to changes comfortably is an important aspect of resilience. Some children seem born to adapt with very little effort. As babies, they are easy to care for and to comfort. New foods and new routines are no problem. Later, strange situations do not usually evoke tears. When such a toddler falls down and bloodies a knee, he or she will quickly get up and return to play. So a child may be born with a certain inclination to adjust to change and meet new challenges. But all children must *learn* to be resilient. Researchers believe that a person who copes well under the adverse circumstances of later life has actually been the beneficiary of long (and successful) training in how to manage. A parent's guiding hand plays a major role in the child's development of coping skills.

Regardless of an individual's innate strength, coping is a learned skill. Over time, a child gradually learns how to assess problems realistically, how to foresee potentially disturbing events, how to anticipate the consequences of various courses of action, and how to make choices among them. Even those born at greater risk can become more resilient as they grow and learn the necessary set of skills. Some children do, though, need extra help through the explicit guidance of their parents. The more a parent helps a child learn to delay acting on impulse, the more time the child is encouraged to take for reflection before action, the less likely the child is to stumble in life. With parental help and support, especially through the medium of family communication, the child learns to gain control both of self and environment, and to become more positive in emotional outlook.

One of the most important coping skills is learning to face and tolerate unpleasant emotions. For an adoptee, perhaps the most unpleasant emotions of early life are the feelings of loss associated with the change that adoption brings. Parents have many opportunities to communicate ways of coping with that bad feeling—with or without words.

The scene is an ordinary one. A parent and child approach the security check in an airport. Gilbert Deaver and his four-year-old son Willy were catching a plane for Grandmother's Thanksgiving dinner. It was a special chance for father and son to spend some time together on their own; Mrs. Deaver, buried under the final stages of preparing to chair a major professional conference, would not be able to join them until the following day. Willy was large for his age, but the big boy unabashedly clutched his teddy bear, eyeless and embarrassingly scruffy of fur, tight to his chest. Where he went, so did the teddy.

When they entered the lane of the metal detector, Willy, at his father's urging, reluctantly permitted his bear to go on the conveyor belt into the mysterious dark box of the x-ray machine. Seconds later, the child burst into a loud wail, and he didn't stop crying even when the bear was safely back in his arms. Passersby stared at the small dapper man and his sturdy son, who would not be comforted. Finally, Gilbert simply knelt down, right there on the airport floor in the middle of the throng. He put his arms around Willy and his teddy and hugged them both. Spectators smothered sympathetic smiles as they hurried past the pair. Willy gave his father a few angry glares, as if he held him personally responsible for the separation from his teddy, but soon the boy's sobs subsided. Finally, Gilbert stood up, took his son's hand, and walked on toward their gate.

Words had failed Gilbert, but he managed, through his simple action, to demonstrate to his son that the child's feelings were worthy of respect. The comfort of a father's touch also made it clear to Willy that the frightening change was over and no harm had been done. In recounting the incident to his wife the following evening, Gilbert confessed, "The truth is, I couldn't figure out what the matter was. I mean, he had his bear back." A child as young as Willy can seldom explain what is the matter, but perhaps in this instance his distress had two roots: his sense of time and his memory of the past. It is sometimes hard to remember that a child's time sense is not like an adult's. The abrupt disappearance of his bear into the x-ray machine could have seemed to last an eternity in Willy's perception. And the disappearance might have reminded the boy that he, too, was separated from his adoptive mother. (In his mind, she was the one who went away, not himself.) Of course, Willy had been previously separated from another mother, which made his adoptive mother's absence all the more painful. He had been 18 months old when placed with the Deavers. Even though Willy at four appeared to have forgotten his earlier attachment, that was likely more apparent than real. Although the boy had probably been too young at the time of his adoption to retain concrete memories, he retained a kind of emotional residue of the memories of his earlier experience in another family—memories that were painfully aroused when a separation, however brief, was experienced again later.

It is easy to recognize that the child who is suddenly in physical pain needs and wants comforting. The adopted child may have an even greater need for reassurance because of memories of that initial experience of loss and sadness, the separation from the first family. Memories have an odd way of remaining. They are like icebergs, with only the tip above water to reveal their presence.

Luz Garcia was three years old when she came to her adoptive family. She had made the adjustment well, and developed into an articulate and athletic youngster. Luz was eleven when she suffered a broken wrist in a softball game after school. Taken to the hospital emergency room, she waited alone for a doctor's attention. A thoughtful nurse called the girl's mother at her office, and Mrs. Garcia spoke to her daughter on the phone. She could hear that Luz was crying, just a little, and she reassured her that she was leaving immediately for the hospital. Sniffling, Luz asked, "What would happen to a child whose mother cannot come when they get hurt?" Her mother sensed that the frightened girl was trying to hold on to the telephone contact. So she responded soothingly, "I am sure you are very scared. The broken bone must hurt a lot. But I'll be right there. The drive is a short one and I am leaving right now."

Mrs. Garcia paused a moment, then asked, "Honey, are you still crying?" Luz bravely answered, "No." Mrs. Garcia added, "I don't want to hang up while you are still upset. Are you sure it's okay?" Her words told Luz that her mother was there for the girl. Through her calm patience on the telephone and later at the hospital, she helped to restore her daughter to a more comfortable state of being. And she presented to Luz a positive model of coping in a difficult moment.

Possessing one's mother is something most children can take for granted. Even a child who is not well loved knows that he or she once owned mother, for the child was entitled to mother's body itself for a safe passage into the world. A child raised in a biological family still owns that experience of mother, even if she is not available emotionally. This sense of possessing the original mother may be missing from the adoptee's life. In its place may come a certain humiliation and fear that is exacerbated when an accident happens, as it did to Luz. As Mrs. Garcia did, an adoptive mother can repair the hurt and soothe the frightened feelings of the child by communicating the message, "I am here."

Learning to Let Go

The resilient child is one who has learned to "let go." That meaning being able to turn one's attention fully on one's present life and away from the past, whether happy or sad. Letting go can be particularly difficult when the past contains memories that are sad, worrisome, and angry. These feelings are intensely painful and children, like adults, try to avoid them. An adoptee who has memories of life in a previous family, with birth parents or foster parents, may feel a great deal of pain from those memories. The ways the child attempts to avoid that pain may be difficult for adoptive parents to handle. But when parents can accept the child's attempts, no matter how misguided, the child eventually becomes strong enough to face the truth. Only then can the past be let go.

Mary Lou was born in Korea. She had been brought to the United States and adopted by Dick and Bunny Sirota when she was five. The identity of her birth father had never been known. Her birth mother had left the girl in a Korean orphanage and disappeared when Mary Lou was only three.

Nine-year-old Mary Lou enjoyed watching TV after school while she helped her mother in the kitchen. They would turn on the evening news while they were getting dinner ready. Her mother noticed that natural disasters, such as earthquakes and floods, particularly fascinated, and simultaneously distressed, the little girl. Even after her mother suggested she stop watching those news stories, Mary Lou continued to watch silently with a horrified expression. Bunny tried to comfort her daughter by pointing out that only a minuscule percentage of the earth's population would be affected by a particular disaster, but that did not alleviate the child's distress.

"Eventually, I figured out what was going on with her," explained Bunny later. After a particularly disturbing shot of an earthquake-devastated city in Mexico, Mary Lou expressed the belief that her parents had died together in a similar earthquake in Korea. That, of course was not the case, as Mary Lou "knew." That is, she knew but she didn't know, as she put it herself when talking about it after she was grown up. Her belief that her birth parents were dead and that they had died together, as a couple, provided a channel through which to mourn her birth mother's loss and the total absence of any information about her birth father. It also gave her somewhere to put the other bad feelings she had about her early life, most especially the hurt and anger that came from thinking that her birth mother had not cared enough to keep her. Mary Lou's scrupulously honest parents were privately distressed by their daughter's fiction, but they wisely chose to remain silent, thereby communicating their support for Mary Lou's feelings. "They put up with it," she smiled ruefully, "until I was finally ready to face the awful truth." And that made it possible then for Mary Lou to let go at long last.

Part of the resilience gained in growing up comes from developing a sense of self control. With parental support, and the chance to talk things over in the family, a child becomes ever more able to cope with feelings of frustration that life inevitably brings—and eventually to do so without depending on one's parents each time for help. With the right kind of help, every youngster can do well. Even the child with special problems can learn this kind of maturity, sometimes even better than others who never faced any real problems. When that happens, the child's achievement exemplifies the possibility that children who are born weak may become strong, despite (or through) their adversity.

Aiysha's parents knew when they adopted her that she had suffered some degree of brain damage at birth. In grade school, she could learn to write only by putting her words on paper in circles rather than horizontal lines. Her language disability also made it hard for her to grasp abstract concepts. She needed to hear even simple ideas repeated many times before she could take them in, or remember them. Among her other problems was a difficulty in copying words from a book or blackboard onto her paper, which made the process of learning even slower. Yet, thanks to the support of her parents and teachers, and her own determination, Aiysha grew up with an adequate facility with the written word.

Aiysha also had another problem characteristic of those who are brain-damaged at birth: an inability to stop and reflect before taking an action, and a difficulty with controlling her anger. When she reached puberty, these tendencies seemed to intensify. Frequently she erupted into major temper tantrums. She also began to steal as an act of vengeance, to "pay back" whomever in the family she was mad at, be it her parents, her older brother, or her younger sister.

Aiysha's parents, Mike and Letty, tried to talk to their daughter about this problem. But after their many attempts seemed to yield little result, they realized that their daughter actually was missing out on much of what was being said in family talks. The other family members were all highly verbal, and Letty in particular typically spoke at a rapid clip, with an extensive vocabulary. It proved to be well nigh impossible for Letty to slow herself down, although she tried valiantly. Aiysha was not only failing to catch the meaning of much that was said in the family, unless it was repeated a number of times, but even when she did catch on, she quickly forgot. That was not because of any deliberate willfulness on her part but a true inability to cope, that derived from her neurological deficit. Her rages continued unabated.

For quite a time, the atmosphere in the house was tense. Fortunately, Mike ultimately had an idea that worked. Daughter and mother would jointly keep a journal. In it, each would record her own ideas about what was wrong and how to fix it. Each would then read the other's entry, at some time when she was calm and by herself. Both Letty and Aiysha were willing to try. The procedure turned out to be especially helpful to Aiysha, because she could slowly go over and over Letty's written words, until they finally became integrated in her mind. Having the words in writing afforded her the extra time she needed to master the concepts. Writing in the journal was helpful to Letty, too, for the activity slowed her down, and she was able to present her thoughts and feelings in a simpler vocabulary and sentence structure than she regularly used in her speech.

Even with the journal as an outlet, Aiysha's temper could still get the better of her. Several times she tore the joint journal apart in a rage. Letty would later rescue the poor book, carefully tape the pages back together, and continue to write in it. "My feelings were hurt, naturally," she admitted, but she was persistent, and her husband gave her the support she needed. As the years of Aiysha's adolescence went on, she became more and more able to contain her anger. Writing about what was wrong and having her words read by her mother, an action that symbolized how hard Letty was trying to understand her daughter, made it increasingly unnecessary for Aiysha to explode. She developed the writing habit to such an extent that she began to keep another, separate, journal in the old-fashioned way, just for herself. And she also became an inveterate writer of notes and letters, proudly avoiding her formerly heavy use of the family telephone. Her friends, relatives, and teachers looked forward to receiving Aiysha's frequent written communications, and she became known and admired in her circle for her habit of writing. When she was eighteen, her parents proudly noted that the child who once could not even write in a straight line had grown up to be a writing person.

Guiding or Controlling?

Sometimes parents try to guide their children by attempting to regulate their thoughts and feelings. That method is particularly undesirable where the adopted child is concerned. A child who had never eaten shrimp before asked for it at a restaurant. Her mother refused to let the girl order it. "I know you won't like it," she explained. "How do you know?" asked the child, with a hint of sulkiness in her voice. (She and her mother had been through this routine before.) "Because I know you better than you know yourself," her mother answered firmly. The child gave in, unable to battle her mother's adamant stand. This girl's mother characteristically presented her own point of view in a way that did not permit her daughter any space in which to exercise her own thought or judgment, or find things out for herself. The mother would not share her power to order from the menu with her daughter, and the child ate a hamburger for lunch that day.

The child's name was Cassie, and she had not been adopted until she was four years old. She had originally been part of her biological family, with a father, mother, and older brother. Sadly, her mother slipped into heavy alcoholism shortly after the little girl's birth. When she deserted the family several years later, Cassie's father, too, began to drink heavily and soon lost his job. He arranged for the youngsters to go to an adoptive home. After visiting them there several times, he disappeared.

In her biological family's home, Cassie had been a cheerful child. Her mother's alcoholism had not seemed to interfere with the child's development; indeed, she delighted in helping her mother as best she could, from early on. Even after she lost both her parents, Cassie was lucky in being placed with her older brother, to whom she was strongly attached. Her adoptive parents had two older biological children, and everyone was happy to include the two "little ones" in their family. Her adoptive mother could not remember anything problematic about the children's initial adjustment; Cassie and her brother seemed to fit in easily and quickly. It was a home with old-fashioned values. "Children should be seen and not heard. Obey and don't ask questions:" these maxims reflected the philosophy of the parents. Like most human beings, they were not always consistent, but they were kind and affectionate parents. Cassie, eager to please and with her altruistic behavior already markedly developed, became "Mother's little helper," sticking close to her adoptive mother, helping with the household chores, and later becoming the older woman's companion and confidante.

But Cassie paid a price for her devotion to her adoptive family's point of view about how she should think and feel. Their desire to regulate her mental life sprang from good intentions, based primarily on their concern that she not be burdened with the pain of the breakup of her biological family. Frequently they pointed out to her, "What is over is over. Don't think about it any more." But her adoptive parents did not realize that memory is never really wiped out, it simply goes underground, remaining hidden in the dark reaches of the mind. In Cassie's case, "forgetting" also meant giving up the happy memories of the loving times with her biological family when they were all together. That is the way memories are, the bad ones take the good with them.

Cassie was left with only one memory of her early life in the time before she was adopted. It was what is often called a "screen memory," not an accurate memory of actual events but a distorted construct. Though it seemed very real to her, Cassie's memory was a distortion of events that had actually happened when her father left her in the care of her new family. The memory went this way: "I was wearing my winter clothing, leggings and princess-style coat. I think I was with someone, my brother maybe, but I'm not sure. Anyway, we were going somewhere, and I was carrying a suitcase. I put it up on my head to carry. It was locked, and the key was already lost. But I knew it was not full of toys or clothes. Only bricks . . . it was full of bricks, and each one was wrapped in foil. That's all I remember."

A screen memory, although distorted, can be examined to see how its symbols point to the truth of a life. Most of the facts of Cassie's memory had to be wrong, but the distortions represented the youngster's actual *lost* memories. Like the foil-wrapped bricks, Cassie's memories were locked away inside her somewhere, and the key to them was gone.

It would have been better for Cassie if her adoptive parents had refrained from interfering with her process of memory. Left to her own devices, she would have forgotten what she wanted to forget and kept only what she wanted to remember. That legacy, even though much of it would probably have been sad, could have supported her feeling of the wholeness of her self. As it was, it seemed that her life must have started at the age of four years. It was as if the earlier part was simply nonexistent, as if she had no babyhood whatsoever.

Children are constantly exposed to changes within and without their bodies. While brushing her teeth, an adolescent girl notices with pleasure the increasing density and shapeliness of her eyebrows. Returning for the new season of Little League practice, a boy of ten exults in the increased speed of his pitch. But not every change arouses joy. A change from the familiar can be painful, and when a child has earlier experienced a deep sadness—as would an adopted child who had to let go of her first love attachment—a change away from something as simple as a satisfying daily routine can reactivate sadness. The young child may not be able to say what is happening, but behavior that is out of the ordinary will show that something is wrong.

Long-legged Gail was four years old. She could already ride her tricycle with great skill and was too big for her beloved stroller. Her parents told the story of how, only weeks before Gail entered nursery school, they had finally decided her stroller had to go. For two days afterward, the little girl would not budge from the back porch steps, where she sat and stared intently at the garage doors, because she knew her stroller was now behind them, joining a mound of family discards. They said she literally just sat there for every minute of two entire days. Her mother, who decided not to interfere with whatever emotions the child was working out, even had to bring lunch out to her.

While she sat, Gail mourned, thinking intently of the loss of her stroller and what it meant to her. How she would never again have that special feeling of being wheeled along the street by her mother. How she would never again make the journey with the older woman as she ran her errands, never again look up to see the sunlight on her mother's hair, coming through the leaves of the trees overhead to bounce around on her mother's face.

Obviously, Gail's parents had not expected how hard it would be for the little girl to let go of the stroller and all it represented. Had they understood how she might feel, especially at a time when the prospect of going to school was already introducing a feeling of change in the child's life, they would have handled the putting away of the stroller differently. They might, for example, have permitted the stroller to remain in a corner of the child's bedroom where she could have seen it whenever she wished. It could have been used for holding Gail's dolls when she wasn't playing with them. It should have been removed only when the child said she was ready to let it go. Perhaps at that time it could have been suggested that she give it to a younger child. In that case, Gail would have let it go proudly, triumphant in the feeling that she did not need to hold on to this symbol of attachment to her mother, that she could be giving now to a smaller child, just as her mother had been giving to her. Being like her mother would soften the loss of her strolls with mother, because she would have gained the loving mother attitude itself, adding that to the rest of her developing capacities.

Guiding a Child Away from Incest Fantasies

All children play roles in the family. The Good Child and the Bad Child are among the most common roles for children. How well the adopted child plays the role that adoptive parents desire is a sign of coping skill. However, the demands of a role can backfire and cause a youngster problems.

When parents actively do not get along, or when their feelings for one another have drained away (though they get along superficially) a child may come to be a special companion to the (needy) parent of the opposite sex. In many ways, the child begins to replace the spouse, offering advice and emotional support, making commitments of time and companionship. The needy parent treats the child more and more as an equal. The unfortunate result is that the youngster's sense of being a child diminishes, or is lost entirely. This scenario can also be true of the single parent family, and the same caution applies. A growing child needs a parent, not a partner. The adoptee's need may be even stronger than another child's because of the loss of the original parents.

A parent must be careful not to communicate marital needs to the child. When the youngster is an adolescent, it is not unusual that incest fantasies can be stimulated by a parent who unwittingly places the child in a partnership role. Fifteen-year-old Norris felt a special closeness to his adoptive mother and she toward him. Temperamentally, they were very much alike. They had the same quick energy, explosive exuberance, and artistic talents and interests. Norris's adoptive father, by contrast, though a reader and active in sports, was often rather withdrawn and melancholic. The parents had grown apart emotionally over the years. Yet, in spite of his closeness to his adoptive mother, Norris suddenly began to claim to his friends that he was really blood related to his father. At home, he said only that he wanted to spend more time with his father and less with his mother. Hearing that, his mother's feelings were hurt, and she withdrew slightly from Norris, doing more of her activities by herself. In seeking closeness to his adoptive father, Norris was unknowingly trying to deal with his sexual fantasies about his mother, and his strategy was successful. The attraction he felt for his mother did not bother him when they were less frequently in one another's presence.

The experience of sexual fantasies in adolescents—adopted or not—toward their parent of the opposte sex may not be uncommon, and can occur without stimulation of the type Norris' mother inadvertently gave. They are easier for an adoptee to cope with, however, if the youngster has lived with the adoptive family since infancy. That boy or girl responds to the parent-child

relationship in much the same way as a youngster growing up in the biological family. The prohibition of conscious sexual feelings towards parents and siblings is
strong and can usually be taken for granted. The youngster who was adopted when older may have more of a
problem. Parents may find that the youngster either
behaves in a sexually provocative way or altogether
avoids the parent or sibling of the opposite sex. Such a
youngster would probably benefit from a discussion
about the issue with the parent of the same sex. However,
if this is hard to initiate, or does not have satisfactory
results, parents should consider seeking help from
professional sources.

Parents in their turn, whether biological or adoptive,
are also subject to feelings of attraction toward their
children, especially as they develop into young women
and men. Like any other parent, the adopter must face
these feelings, so that the child is not burdened by their
expression. Even though much might be deeply buried
beneath the surface of family life, talking it over as a
couple helps lighten parents' problems. One mother told
another in a support group, "Our Jennie and Jimmy are
two absolutely gorgeous kids, and I can't help wanting
to touch them all the time. My husband says he feels the
same way, especially toward Jennie. Of course, as the
children are getting older. . . ." Her voice trails off. "How
do you handle it?" asked the group leader. "We just tell
each other hands off!" the woman answered. She and her
husband had used the power of communication to help
each other cope with a potentially difficult situation, and
avoid expressing their feelings in ways that might be
harmful to their adoptive children.

Playing the "Bad Child" Role

In the adoptive family, the usual secrecy and lack of information about a child's birth and background create fertile ground in which the imagination of the adoptive parent can construct a "Bad Child" image. Adoptive parents are prone to do this when their baby behaves in ways that don't meet their expectations, or that are hard to understand or accept. An infant's screaming rages, for example, may be of special concern to a parent who is quiet and comes from a placid family background. Certain symptoms of adjustment difficulties in an older child, such as bedwetting, lying, and stealing, may also frighten parents who are anxious about their child's biological heritage. Yet, generally speaking, these behaviors are not only common but usually transient. They respond quickly to help and guidance from the parents, and from professionals when necessary.

Genetic inheritance is one component of every child's personality, and some children may inherit a tendency or weakness that sooner or later might show up in antisocial behavior or other serious psychological disturbance. For example, children are believed to be at risk for alcoholism if there is alcoholism in their genetic background. But tendencies are no more than that. They can be handled and headed off by parents who inform themselves about the situation, understand it, and are not afraid. This is true whether children are raised in a biological or adoptive family. For example, if there is reason to believe a child is at risk for developing alcoholism, the parents need to think through how to handle and restrict the use of alcoholic beverages in their home. The family may also want to seek professional guidance for help in dealing with such problems and apprehensions.

Adoptive parents, of course, often face the challenge of not knowing exactly what their child's genetic inheritance may be. That ignorance may cause the parents needless anxiety, but it can also provide a kind of freedom that allows the child to develop as an individual, without the constriction of preconceived notions or roles. These can be damaging to a child, even with the best of parental intentions. Caroline, a mother raising her biological son Scott, does so with some trepidation. She has heard from her husband's relatives that Scott's particular combination of red hair, blue eyes, and hot temper has over the generations been associated with problem personalities. As her sister-in-law put it, "It spells trouble! Why, Great-uncle Jack even went to jail for a while!" So, as Scott screams wildly for the ball he threw out of his crib and cannot reach, Caroline asks herself apprehensively if he will grow up to be one of the wild ones. In other words, she has already begun to typecast her son as a bad child. His growing awareness of her attitude will affect the boy, and in time he is likely to feel a sense of lowered self-esteem. The worst result could be that he finally learns to play the role of Bad Child, just as she feared.

There is an important difference between Scott's position and that of an adoptee who manifests traits a parent may interpret as "bad." Scott has blood relatives that he can know, or know about, with whom he can feel a strong sense of identification. As Scott matures and learns to cope with various kinds of adverse situations, he will eventually be able to say to himself, "Well, Great-uncle Jack does have a bad temper, but he is also a good man, in spite of that brief jail sentence for getting into a fist fight with a traffic cop. Everyone in the family loves him. After all, it isn't that bad that I am like him." Scott can comfort himself about his future because he has a model who is good as well as bad.

The adopted child has no such recourse. In the imagination of the child (and perhaps the adoptive parent as well) there is nothing to counterbalance the negative model that has been created. The adoptee has no one to feel identified with as a total human being, and therefore may feel a loss of self-esteem. Membership in an adoptive group may provide support for the family communication required to deal with this kind of situation. The group may help to remind parents that they have many ways of helping and teaching their children to cope with unpleasant emotions. Willy's father comforted his boy silently, with a hug. Luz's mother had helped the girl get through the trauma of a broken wrist by just being there, and by saying so. Mary Lou's parents wisely chose to communicate their support by not contradicting the story she made up. Aiysha's father was a facilitator and a peacemaker, who helped his wife and daughter use the written word when spoken words failed. These are all examples of successful communication that gently guided a child toward learning how to handle adversity and develop resilience.

6 Self Esteem: Measuring Up

When adolescents ask, "Who am I?" their thoughts are of the future. They want positive answers to questions about the lifestyle and mode of work they are headed toward, the kind of family they will create for themselves. They want to know if they will like themselves when they become adults. For adolescent adoptees, the question "Who am I?" has a second, equally important, time dimension. For them, the question applies not just to their future, but also to their unknown past—and their unknown birth parents.

Puberty's growth spurt is a powerful signal that adult decisions and commitments are about to make their demands. No longer does the "good child" ideal impel behavior as it once did. Undeviating loyalty to parents' approved ways of thought and behavior loses its strength. Even so, the gratifications of nurturing by Mom and Dad and the security sensed from their moral leadership do not simply vanish. To the adolescent, parents unwittingly represent a dangerous, if largely unacknowledged, temptation. Unintentionally, they stimulate the teen's wish to return to the pleasures and safety of childhood. The activities that parents decry—rock concerts, bizarre grooming, even experimentation with drugs (not to condone a dangerous practice but to place it in the adolescent perspective) help adolescents mark off and maintain their single-minded passage toward the autonomy of adulthood. In the struggle to find an answer to the question, "Who am I?", some young people will remain undecided and conflicted into their thirties. Others will have done with it, for better or for worse, before they graduate from high school. The majority will find a satisfactory resolution in their early twenties.

Am I (Not) Good Enough?

To feel comfortable about the hard certainties of the near future and the soft unknowns of the more distant future, it helps to be at ease in facing the value judgments implicit in the question, "Who am I?" Not only, "Am I a good person?" (beautiful, smart, talented) in the eyes of others, but also the more agonizing question, "Am I (not) good enough in their eyes?"

No matter how much recognition comes from family, friends, and peers, it is hard for the adoptee to feel as confident as other children about having a "good enough" self. The most ordinary events of life can stimulate painful fantasies created to deal with the unanswerable question, "Why was I given away?" Of that event that turns the natural order of things on its head, no explanation is ever fully acceptable—not as it concerns the feelings of the person given away.

Fortunately, as the adoptee matures, it becomes possible to set fantasy aside and accommodate valid explanations that are presented in a positive way. Most adolescents can and do become skilled at the strategy of differentiating between thoughts dominated by wishes and/or anxiety, and thoughts motivated by logic, especially when they can rely on good communication within the family. Good communication, along with parental support and unconditional love, heals the grievous hurt enough to allow needed energy to be saved for the road ahead.

An example of an ordinary event that for the adoptee recalls the original wound is simply having to produce a birth certificate. By its very existence, the adoptee's certificate, amended from the original, announces to the world that a child was once given away. "I wanted to crawl into a hole and fall straight through to China," said Mabel of her first application for a passport at the busy Rockefeller Center office in New York City. "I was 21 years old and planning my first trip to Europe. It was late on a summer Friday afternoon, the line had been horrendous, it took two and a half hours to reach the clerk. Suddenly, it seemed like she was taking an awfully long time to look over my birth certificate. For a moment, I was sure she was going to turn me down." Mabel sighed. "Silly, isn't it? Here I am, several years older, and I still have anxious feelings about that experience. I knew even then, of course, that I wasn't being rational. Maybe the clerk was exhausted, like me, or maybe my certificate caught her interest because she hadn't seen one like it before. Who knows? Maybe she was a kindred soul, adopted herself!"

Mabel thought that the feelings she had about her birth certificate might never go away. She had recently spoken to adoptees twenty years her senior who still felt just as she did. She went on to emphasize that it had nothing to do with her adoptive family. "I had a loving home . . . ," her voice trailed away and she sighed again. She said she had told her family how she felt that day at the passport office. Her supportive parents had assured her that they thought they would feel the same way in her situation. That type of response comforts an adoptee, because it creates a sense of solidarity with their experience. The other common approach that well-meaning relatives sometimes take, to say that the matter is unimportant, does not really give comfort. What that statement means to the adoptee is only that the other person does not consider the matter important and does not understand how the adoptee feels.

Young Joe Morell had an experience of a different kind with his birth certificate when he was thirteen. Joe's adoptive parents, both journalists, had accepted an assignment in a part of Africa that was without regular communication to the outside world. While they were away, Joe stayed with his mother's parents in the midwest. There, the local authorities would not allow him to enroll in school until proof positive could be provided of his identity. It was a reasonable request, at a time when fears had been roused nationwide over kidnapped and abducted children. Even though Joe's grandparents were well-known in their community, the principal explained that he could not bend the rules.

The problem was that Joe's birth certificate was carefully laid away in a safety deposit box in a New York bank. In order to obtain it, his parents would have to be notified in Africa; they in turn would have to contact their bank; the red tape governing the opening of the safety deposit box without their presence would have to be negotiated. Until all that could take place, Joe was excluded from school. Joe's problem could have happened to anybody, adopted or not, but for the adoptee, it had a special meaning. The importance of his (amended) birth certificate seemed heavily emphasized.

Joe's problem was finally solved when it occurred to Joe's grandparents that the principal of his New York school might be able to vouch for his identity. Joe was then accepted at school without the additional weeks of waiting it would have taken to get his birth certificate. In looking back on this situation years later, Joe recalled, "I liked the extra vacation. But when I saw the other kids going to school, I felt like I was Mr. Nobody. Don't ask me why, I know it wasn't logical. The school had a right to ask for my birth certificate, but to me it was like rubbing salt in a wound." He added, "My grandfather made me feel okay though. He said, 'I am a grandfather because you are my grandson. You are *not* a Mr. Nobody.'"

Joe's grandfather had conveyed the idea that, "We are in this together." His wise response emphasized his own feeling that Joe's very existence, his being alive in the world, gave the older man satisfaction and fulfillment through their relationship, even though it was not biological. For the boy, it helped to make up for the bad feelings that came with the thought that he was a member of the family because he had been given away by another family—the implicit message in an adoptee's amended birth certificate.

Questions About Self-Worth

Initial questions in regard to self-worth often arise before the pre-teen years. At that age, youngsters observe the world around them carefully, and compare themselves with others. They make comparisons of their neighborhood, house, clothing, and family car with those of their age mates; they also compare their own talents and achievements with those of their classmates. An adoptee's observations are like those of other children, but in addition, there is the circumstance of being adopted to puzzle over. What does it mean so far as one's personal value is concerned? Thus, a taken-for-granted event in another child's life, such as the birth of a sibling, can be the stimulus for painful self-scrutiny and fantasizing. That is what happened when eight-year-old David learned his adoptive parents were going to have their first biological child.

David had been adopted a few weeks after his birth by Marnie and Noel. When he was not quite three, he participated in the family's joy over the adoption of his baby sister Sandra. David grew into a bright and fearless little boy, showing about the normal amount of rivalry with his sister. He viewed his adoptive status matter-of-factly. On rare occasions, he had asked questions about his "other mother," seeming to think of her as some distant relative he had never met. But that was about to change.

After Marnie had become unexpectedly pregnant—not an uncommon occurrence for adoptive parents who had thought they were infertile—she and her husband told David and Sandra about the impending arrival of the baby, and were careful to include the children in all their plans for the new arrival. The first hint that David's good feelings about himself were changing came when he and Sandra (a less assertive child than her brother, and his devoted copycat) let Marnie know that they objected to the books about baby care she was reviewing in the evening. Marnie was puzzled, for the books were the same ones she had read to prepare for David's entry into the family, but she agreed to postpone her reading until after David and Sandra were in bed.

Marnie did not want to let this important issue pass without further family conversation. She insisted, "I think there is more to it than just the books. I think something is bothering you. Right?" Neither child responded. After reiterating her statement and receiving no further explanation of their cryptic request, Marnie concluded lamely, "Perhaps you'll tell me more later, when you feel more like it." Marnie assumed that the children had some feelings about the expected birth, but as she said, "I didn't want to act like a mind reader, to be the type of parent who always knows what's in the children's minds better than they know themselves." So she gave them time to reflect, and to digest her interpretation of their response. In that way, she could teach them that problems can be worked out through reflection and family communication.

But the children did not bring up the subject again. Nevertheless, on an afternoon several weeks later, when Marnie and her son were alone in the house, she learned more. The two were sitting companionably at opposite ends of the long kitchen table. Marnie was peeling vegetables for a savory stew, David was industriously looking over his geography homework. He asked his mother to name the capital of Rhode Island, and teased her when she couldn't think of it. Then, without preamble, the boy introduced a new subject. He blurted out, "Why did my other mother give me up?" In describing the moment later, Marnie said she had not been prepared for her son's quick change of mood, but she offered him again the explanation he had already been given. It was the best one that she knew: that both his birth parents had been very young and lacked the capability to make a home for a child at that time in their lives. David persisted, "Then why did she have me?" Marnie answered, "I don't think she knew she would have a baby when she was having intercourse." David responded, "I know that, Mommy, but why does it it still hurt?"

Marnie reported that she lost her breath for a moment, as she herself shared her son's deep feelings of hurt. David looked down at the map he had been drawing. She wanted to comfort him but did not know what to say. It seemed that the hypothetical statements she had given David when he was younger were no longer satisfying to him. Marnie did not try to reassure David at that moment that his adoptive family loved him. He had known that all his life, and she did not think he was questioning it now. Instead, she decided to suggest that he might like to talk about his questions with another adoptee, an older person who had gone through the same feelings. It would not be difficult to arrange, for the family was active in adoptive circles in their community, and Marnie knew that any of the adolescents would gladly take the role of buddy to a younger adoptee. Sharing one's thoughts and feelings can be as comforting at eight as it is at eighteen or eighty. By her suggestion, Marnie let David know that she respected the uniqueness of his questions about the motivations of his birth parents, and that the question of why he was alive in the world had value.

David was silent for a moment after his mother's suggestion. Then he asserted, "No, Mommy, when I am a little older, when I am not so shy about talking about it, then you can find me somebody to talk to." He meant shy about discussing his adoptive status outside the family; otherwise, David was not shy about anything. So Marnie did not arrange for her son to talk to an older boy. Once David had aired the bad feelings he had about himself as a given-away child, he became uninterested in further talk about it. Just knowing he could talk about a subject almost unspeakable seemed enough of an emotional support for the school-age youngster. David was then free to continue to concentrate his energies on his positive interests—studies, sports and friends.

David's baby sister, Lorraine, was born several months after his talk with his mother. As he and his father were bending over the newborn's crib admiring her on a Sunday morning, David expressed himself in a tone of wonderment. "So that's what it's like! She's so tiny!"

"Yes," echoed Noel. "It's always like that. You were like that when we brought you home." The two punched each other playfully in the shoulder as they went outside to shoot a few baskets.

Another ordinary event that has special meaning for an adoptee is losing a pet. Every pet owner feels the pain of having to say goodbye to a beloved cat or dog, but the youngster who was given away once feels the pain in an especially intense way. Nine years old and a city dweller, Charlotte Sanders, who came into her adoptive family just a few days after her birth, had always felt unconditionally accepted by her parents. She also had a dog that she loved dearly. Tillie was her "baby." Unfortunately, Tillie had a tendency to bite and little discrimination about her victims. The family had quickly learned to be cautious in approaching her, but the dog also tried to nip unsuspecting visitors, both adults who came to see the parents and children who came to see Charlotte and her older brother. After years of trying to cope with the problem of Tillie, the Sanders eventually decided that, for the safety of all, Charlotte's dog would have to be given away to friends who had a house in the country. There Tillie could live in the yard, and her biting propensities would be less troublesome. Charlotte reacted to this sensible decision with enormous anguish and angry tears. She said to her parents, "Would you give me away? What if something were wrong with me? I will never forgive you if you give Tillie away!"

Charlotte deeply identified with the dog she had had as long as she could remember; in that, she was like many pet owners. But unlike pet owners who are not adopted, she also identified her pet with that other part of her self, the part that was not of the Sanders family, that mysterious and unknown beginning that had opened with what she obviously felt had been an unforgivable act, that of giving her away. Behind the question directed to the future, what if something were to be wrong with me, hid a more pressing concern about the past: what if she had been given away because they (her birth parents) had found something wrong with her?

Like other teenage adoptees who are basically well-adjusted and happy youngsters, Charlotte carried deep inside her an inexplicable sense of loss. It was not a feeling she ever put into words. Indeed, she would not have been aware of it at all, except that it crystallized in this situation which demanded that she let go of something to which she was deeply attached. That caused a subtle lowering of her usual good feelings about her life and herself. She found the implication of the idea, "I was given away once," so distressing that she turned it around, making her adoptive parents into the bad parents who would give away a child (Tillie). At that moment, they represented the original bad parents, her birth parents, who had marked her as bad—which is how she felt, even though she did not ordinarily think of herself as bad.

Charlotte's parents realized they had confronted their daughter with a practical issue for which she was not yet ready. So they did not insist that her dog be given away. As it turned out, Tillie lived with the family for the rest of her life. They habituated themselves to taking precautions to protect their visitors. As for Charlotte, she became able to view the behavior of her parents and others from more than one perspective as she grew older, and that made life and "letting go" when necessary easier for her. But the fact that her parents had not insisted on giving Tillie away had also been important. It meant to her that they really respected and cared about how she felt, although they themselves could never directly experience the feeling.

Selling the family house is another ordinary event with special repercussions for an adoptee. The Brewsters decided to sell theirs when Todd was transferred to a branch office in another part of the state. Their sixteen-year-old daughter Pam, an adoptee, reacted to the event with an unusually sharp sense of pain, the kind that usually comes from an extraordinary loss.

Pam, a pure-blooded American Indian, was a strikingly attractive teenager, with olive skin, high cheekbones, deep brown eyes, and beautiful heavy straight hair as black as coal. She did not in the least resemble her parents, both of whom were blue-eyed blondes. Some youngsters handle the differences of appearance that are obvious in trans-racial adoptions by simply ignoring them. They "see" themselves as they see their parents, taking over their parents' racial identity and displaying pride in it. They seem to "white out" their own heritage. Pam was not one of those children.

The Brewsters had always believed it was important to help their daughter develop a strong sense of her separate racial identity. They feared if she denied her own background she would be divided inwardly and her sense of self would be weakened. Their point of view was in accord with the soundest precepts of child psychology. To support Pam's racial identity and pride, her parents emphasized their multi-ethnic view of life. They lived in a racially integrated community. Mrs. Brewster speculated that she too might have had Indian ancestry, as well as black, because her father was Hispanic. The family talked openly and freely about adoptive issues. But, with all that support and communication, looking different from her parents was a constant reminder to Pam of her lack of biological connection to them. It always made her remember that once she had been given away.

As she was growing up, Pam had developed a deep attachment to the house in which the family lived. She felt it was "special," as in a sense it was, because it was an old Victorian the Brewsters had salvaged and rehabilitated before the restoration movement made that fashionable. Pam particularly loved her own room, under the eaves with dormered windows. Her parents had built her a window seat, where she could sit and look directly into the branches of a crabapple tree that flowered lushly in spring. When she was ten, Pam was thrilled to be allowed to redecorate the room herself, and chose a cheerful yellow and white scheme. The colors were picked up in the flowered wallpaper, in her bedspread, and in the woven rug she and her mother had shopped earnestly to find. When the room was finished, her grandmother announced there would be a special present, a piece of furniture, whatever Pam wanted. After several weeks of consideration, Pam decided on a maple book case. She had also weighed the possibility of a dressing table, but she felt that first her books needed a "home" of their own. Her glass ran over later that year, when her parents gave her a dressing table and stool for Christmas, covered in a yellow and white floral pattern. Pam inevitably brought friends up to see and admire her room. She kept it neat as a pin always, reported her mother about the girl who was in most things sloppy.

Pam fantasized that the whole house, and especially her room, projected her true self. If an inanimate object could be such, her room was surely her twin, or at least a kindred spirit. She said so by way of explaining later her unexpected and disturbing behavior. When she had heard that a buyer had come forward with an acceptable offer for the house, Pam wept bitterly, saying, "How could you do that to me? The house and I came together!" That statement was literally true. Her parents had bought the house at the time they adopted Pam. Brought to it from the hospital where she was born, Pam had never lived anywhere else.

Pam ran away, leaving without a word. The Brewsters frantically notified the police. Two worry-filled days passed before they received a telephone call from one of

Pam's high school friend's, saying their daughter would be home in a few days.

When Pam returned, there were tears and recriminations on both sides. Pam revealed her reason for running away as she rhetorically demanded, "Why did you have to sell the house?" She had wanted to take revenge on her parents for their decision to move. It was as if the house itself were a vulnerable object, and they were acting like bad (birth) parents, getting rid of it. Did they remember that someone got rid of Pam once, too? The earlier information, given Pam by the Brewsters on more than one occasion, that her birth parents had been unmarried and too young to raise a child, had not been forgotten. Those facts just did not mean anything to her at that moment in her life.

Although she did not run away again, Pam took much time and had many talks with her parents before she was able to forgive them. For their part, they had to face the fact that they had hurt Pam's trust in them by their action in selling the house, however necessary it seemed for Todd's career. In retrospect, it was clear that Pam needed a lengthy period of talking out her feelings before she could differentiate between the unknown motivations of her unknown birth parents and the intentions of her adoptive parents in selling the house to move to another community. Fortunately, the Brewsters were able to acknowledge their role in the problem, although they did not condone their daughter's behavior in running away. Their candor helped Pam eventually regain her emotional equilibrium, as well as her trust in the goodness of her adoptive parents.

The issue of abortion, a sensitive matter for many people, is another one that is especially painful for adoptees. As sixteen-year-old Michelle Berton put it, "But for some unknown woman's decision, where would I be?" Michelle was talking to her adoptive mother, Henrietta, about her day at school. She described an upsetting situation in ethics class. The students had been asked to debate the question of abortion, and it turned out that Michelle was the only one to choose an anti-abortion stand. Now she worried that she would get a bad grade for what she saw as her weak defense of the position that struck her as having deep personal relevance. "If only someone who was Catholic had spoken up. . . . All the heat was on me. I blanked out when it was my turn. I couldn't think of anything logical like, 'The Kantian categorical imperative is not fulfilled by the practice of abortion.' I just didn't want to say, 'That could have been me that was thrown away.' "

Her mother first addressed the practical issue worrying her daughter, by pointing out that Michelle was an A student and one low grade was not the end of the world. Then, changing her tone, she challenged Michelle's fantasy. Didn't her very existence mean that her birth mother had obviously wanted Michelle to be born? Henrietta hoped that from her logical hypothesis, her daughter would draw the inference that the issue of abortion and Michelle's being alive were not necessarily connected. But she recognized that it is difficult to comfort an adolescent with the hypothetical approach. The ability of a teenager to evaluate a situation realistically, and to feel pain, are like an adult's. The empty space in one's life story cannot be filled in by a reassurance from adoptive parents. Henrietta knew she was not really making her point successfully, yet she could not actually speak for the unknown woman who was Michelle's birth mother. For her part, Michelle understood that her mother meant well, and she appreciated the concern implicit in the conversation. But she probably also felt that her mother's point was irrelevant to her own feelings of pain.

Shortly afterward, Michelle went to bed with a headache. Her worried parents could only think of one positive step to take to give their daughter some support: to talk to her principal about the ramifications of discussing abortion in the classroom. They wanted to make him aware that beyond the "pro-choice" and "pro-life" stands, there was a third point of view: that of the adoptee. But when they talked to Michelle about it the next morning, she expressed clearly that she was unwilling for them to carry out their plan. She said she did not want her feelings about herself to come under discussion, as it seemed inevitable they would. The privacy of the principal's office was not private enough. Her parents deferred to Michelle's feelings, acknowledging that she was capable of knowing what was best for herself. Michelle did agree that "some day" her parents could speak out. "Maybe I'll have something to say myself one day," she added. And that is how her story came to be included here.

The Bad Seed Fantasy

The question, "Am I (not) good enough?" is sometimes confused by adoptees with questions about the character of their unknown birth parents. When that happens, a period of discomfort results. It may be short-lived and of no lasting consequence, or it may be long

lasting, deeply felt, and intensively self-destructive, requiring professional help for the adolescent to deal with.

Seventeen-year-old Melissa was considered by her
crowd to be very straitlaced. When she was nine weeks
old, she had been adopted by a farm family with funda-
mental religious values. About to graduate from high
school with a straight A record, Melissa was seriously
considering a career in country music. As her participation in high school talent shows indicated, she had the
right kind of voice, wholesome good looks, and an unusual ability to project her personality throughout a
large auditorium. One worry was that such a career
choice would present great temptations, through the
close association of the professional music scene with
drug abuse and sexual opportunism, but Melissa felt
confident she would be able to steer clear of enticements.
Her parents agreed, and made it clear that they approved
of their daughter's ambition to sing out to a world that
needed all the help it could get.

Then Melissa read an unauthorized biography of
Janis Joplin, which told how the singer's life had been
complicated by promiscuity and drug abuse. This book
awakened painful anxieties in Melissa. She had always
wondered if her musical talents were a birth heritage;
now, certain details of the biography raised questions in
her mind about whether her out-of-wedlock birth could
possibly be traced to Janis herself. Melissa noted that the
star was seventeen years older than herself, and remembered that one of the few facts she knew about her birth
mother was that she had been seventeen when Melissa
was born. It all seemed more than coincidence when her
best friend Leila called attention to the fact that Melissa

looked very much like the photo of Janis on the book jacket.

Melissa agreed. "We have the same eyes," she said. Sadly, she added, "But what if I go wrong, like her?" Leila tried to reassure her friend. "You would never do that," she insisted. Melissa shrugged and changed the subject.

In fact, this was not the first time that Melissa had expressed a worry that she might have inherited some undesirable tendencies from her unknown birth parents. The thought had occurred to her before, especially at times when she felt very sensitive about her out-of-wedlock birth. Although her adoptive parents had years earlier explained to Melissa that her adoption made her as "legal" as any other child, she, like many other adopted youngsters, was not entirely convinced. In her community and her church, illegitimacy was heavily stigmatized, and it was inevitable that the innocent child had to bear the brunt of the disapproval. Her adoptive parents had tried to protect Melissa by not revealing the fact that her birth parents were unmarried until she was old enough to cope with the information. Even so, a youngster in Melissa's environment is especially subject to the Bad Seed fantasy. A line from Euripides sums up the fantasy: "A bad beginning makes a bad ending."

Melissa identified herself strongly with her adoptive mother and her mother's religious principles. Psychologically, a growing girl takes in the attitudes of her family, and especially her mother, as materially she takes in the food she is served. Yet Melissa was sensitive about the tendencies she might have inherited, particularly in view of the fact that she had such sparse information about her birth heritage: just the fact of her birth mother's age when Melissa was born, and the knowledge that she was an illegitimate child. Some adopted girls handle their Bad Seed fantasy by acting out the birth mother image they fantasize; they become as promiscuous as they imagine their birth mothers to have been. (Studies indicate that mothers who give their children up for adoption are no more promiscuous than the rest of the population.) Melissa didn't act out her fantasies, but she did suffer inwardly.

Her friend Leila knew that Melissa would never talk to her adoptive parents about these negative feelings, because she would worry that they would in turn be upset. So Leila herself informed Melissa's parents of their daughter's concerns. They decided to seek the advice of their minister. A kindly man whose congregation consulted him freely, he pointed out reflectively that uncertainty about an issue of such critical importance as the personality and circumstances of a birth mother can foster disturbing, although usually groundless, fears. He suggested that the family look into a discussion group, held by a sister church in another community, for adopted young people. He recommended talking things over together as the best strategy for young people. It helps clear their minds when they can communicate freely with other people of their own age.

Buoyed by their pastor's support, Melissa's parents revealed to her that they were aware of her worry, asking her to forgive her best friend for the breach of her confidence. Melissa took the news good-naturedly. Perhaps she felt some relief that her concern was finally out in the open. As it happened, she did visit the discussion group but did not become a regular participant. It was a little too far away, and besides, she had decided to go to college rather than becoming a country singer. She liked the idea, though, that she had a place to go should she ever feel she needed it.

The Bad Seed fantasy of the adopted person has two meanings. It refers to "sinful" biological parents, and to abnormal eggs or sperm that could result in a child who is "not alright." One meaning of the fantasy may be emphasized over the other, but always, when the Bad Seed fantasy is firmly held, it damages the pride of the adoptee.

People in a state of emotional pain usually try to avoid it. One way is through the deliberate use of drugs and alcohol. Another time-honored strategy is taking some sort of action. In the nineteenth century, for example, physicians commonly prescribed world tours for their affluent patients who were suffering from "a broken heart." All unknowing, an adolescent girl who believes that her birth mother was promiscuous may "prescribe treatment" for herself. She acts promiscuously. By acting as she thinks her birth mother did, she no longer feels the shame and anger that the image of her birth mother would otherwise arouse. Yet imagination does not crystallize to the point of such action unless it has been supported by cues in the environment. In Nancy Wong's story, the stimulus was the explanation her adoptive parents gave her of how she came into the family.

Nancy's parents were an older Oriental couple. Her father had a grown son from his first marriage, but his second wife could not conceive a child. Nancy was told that she came into their lives in a very dramatic way. One evening, the Wongs went to an Oriental movie theater, to see a film in their own language. A pretty young woman, holding a baby girl about two months old, slipped into the darkened theater and sat next to Mrs. Wong. Midway through the picture, she tapped the older woman on the shoulder: would she mind watching the baby for a few minutes, while the young woman went to freshen up in the Ladies Room? She handed over the child and then walked away into the darkness. She never returned.

In her pre-adolescent years, Nancy elaborated on the story her parents had told her. Using as evidence her round eyes (actually, not all Orientals have the stereotypical almond eyes) she convinced herself that her birth mother had to have been mixed-race, possibly Hispanic (a group less highly regarded in her community than Orientals). To the fantasy she was building up, Nancy added the belief that her birth mother must have been a prostitute. And finally, she came to believe that her birth mother had become pregnant by her adoptive father. It might have been an accident, when he was just "fooling around," or it might have been some kind of arrangement undertaken because he wanted the child his barren second wife could not conceive. Nancy wasn't sure of the details, but she did succeed in convincing herself that she was the biological daughter of her adoptive father. In her mind, that accounted for the deep sense of affinity she felt with him, as well as the coldness she thought she perceived in her mother's attitude toward her.

Unfortunately, the relationships in the Wong family froze at this point in time. When Nancy was thirteen, her parents were killed in an accident. Until that moment, Nancy had been a model child: bright, pretty, well-behaved, with high marks in school. After the tragic accident, she went to live with her godparents. They were fond of Nancy but failed to observe that her inner world began to fall apart. She continued to maintain her good grades in school, and at home she seemed as docile as ever. But out on the streets, she went wild. She became involved with a group of older Hispanic boys and was flagrantly sexually promiscuous. Eventually, she confided her secret to a trusted teacher, who helped Nancy get into psychotherapy.

During the several years of her treatment, Nancy personally investigated the story she had been told about her adoption. She learned that it was completely fabricated. She had been adopted through a reputable social agency, and there was no record that her birth mother had ever been in contact with either of her adoptive parents. That information came as an explosion in her emotional life, which permitted the dark pool of her damned-up self-denigration to begin to drain. She would have much work to do, both within the treatment sessions and without in the years to come. Even so, Nancy could at last set a course for her future. That it would include honor, hope, and high expectations, she no longer doubted.

7 The Two Heritages

My identity does not start with me. I am the end point. I see a shadowy line of ancestors circling back to the dawn of human history. Shape, size, color, potentials of intellect and emotion—all were bequeathed to me. My race, its culture and destiny, my family and its past history, the flow of interlocking relationships and their goodness that make the present and the future possible: these are my heritage.

And heritage feeds self-worth. The answer to the question of "Who am I?" is rooted in the past. Interest in the heritage of the self seems to peak in late adolescence and early adulthood. But the inchoate sense of self starts for us all in the earliest months of life, even before we are capable of the notion, "This is me!" or "That is mine."

Research into early child development suggests that an infant perceives the self primarily as the physical body, which is for many months after birth still felt as being part of the mother. Not until development of the ability to grasp simple symbols and to use speech does a child seem to recognize that the "piggies" Mother has been so gently drying off after the bath are "Mine! . . . mine! . . . my piggies!" The alert baby, physically and mentally developed to the point of grasping the difference between "me" and "you," squeals in delight at this game with an awareness of the unique self thus defined.

But we never forget the feelings of those early days. The deep sense of one's self as an entity shared with Mother, and of her as the first "heritage" we experience, continues throughout a lifetime. A school-age child will sometimes explain, "I am a boy (or girl) because my mother made me that way." (In actual fact, of course, gender is genetically determined by the father's chromosomes.) Only gradually does that feeling of a shared self slip away from the immediate consciousness. Even an adult who no longer consciously remembers the feeling will pick out a Mother's Day greeting card similar to that once offered by Western Union when its services were a ubiquitous part of the American scene: "All that I am and all that I hope to be, I owe to you, my Mother."

Psychological Heritage

The story of an individual's psychological heritage starts in the womb, when the developing child does most literally possess the mother. After birth, the mother's love for the newborn is soon reciprocated by the baby's feeling of WANTING mother. That quickly translates into another powerful feeling, that of OWNING the Mother who freely gives her love. The reciprocal process that entangles loving, wanting and owning provides the prototype for the formation of the strong family bonds that will come later.

A baby who is taken into the adoptive family at birth overcomes the divided beginning of the mother-child relationship and is able to develop a sense of psychological heritage in the same way as others—from the mother's sheltering arms. Later, the telling may temporarily disrupt that sense, as some of the stories in chapter 3 illustrate. The understanding of the adoptive parents at that time is essential if the hurt is to be minimized and the psychological heritage to remain undivided.

The feeling of ownership of the mother is usually established by about ten months of age. It will reveal its existence in the child's trusting, possessive, even imperious manner toward Mother. Children who are adopted after they are more than a few weeks old will experience some disruption in the development of this feeling and consequently may take longer to develop a feeling of possession. Children who are adopted after toddlerhood will experience additional complications, because they may already have developed a feeling of ownership in regard to the birth mother or a foster mother. Such children experience development of a somewhat different nature, which cannot be easily generalized. The story of Terri later in the chapter tells how it went for one little girl.

Learning the Family History

In a real sense, the adoptee has two heritages, one from the adoptive family and the other from the birth family. Together, they provide the given boundaries, the limitations and potentials of the adopted child's life. It sometimes happens that the heritages are not particu-

larly compatible. An adoptee must always actively work
to integrate them, to create a balance that assures pride
and hope, despite the lack of information about and
connection to the birth family.

Of course, it is not uncommon to know little about
your family heritage. That happens to many people
raised in biological families. The cliche that Americans
are a nation of immigrants means that many of us have
lost sight of earlier generations and know little or nothing about the family's historical past, the time before the
grandfathers and grandmothers. Even those whose ancestors came over on the Mayflower may be cut off from
knowledge of the family past by the peculiarly American
habit of moving constantly from place to place. Few of
us can find more than two generations of headstones in
a single cemetery. Yet, for those who are interested, there
are ways of filling in the missing facts. The search for
one's roots, perhaps with the enthusiastic help of the
local genealogical society, can be an absorbing hobby.
And what isn't known can be filled in by daydreams. A
great-grandmother known to have come from Ireland
can be given a family castle set in a lush green estate;
the vague statement that there is "Indian blood" in the
family creates a picture of a proud warrior wearing eagle
feathers and a bear claw necklace into battle.

Obviously, the adoptee who wants to learn about
the history of the birth family faces a more difficult
challenge. Typically, no facts are available to serve as
the basis for genealogical research. (The organization
ALMA seeks to rectify that omission, by working to
locate and open birth records and to find birth families.
It is open to adoptees over the age of eighteen.) And
daydreaming to flesh out a coherent family history can

create some problems not present for the non-adopted, as the story of Matty later in the chapter exemplifies. Even the adoptee who comes into the adoptive family when older and with the experience of knowing the birth family often confronts a special type of problem in regard to the history of the birth family. The very facts that are known firsthand usually have negative implications: that the birth parents were inadequate care givers; that they came from a lower socioeconomic position than the adoptive family; that they were physically unwell or mentally disturbed. It is not always a blessing to possess information about the birth family. Fortunately, adoptive parents can help their children manage the intricacies of their dual heritage. And good family communication plays an important role in this process.

Taking Your Family for Granted

Ordinary children take their family and home for granted. Home is "where one starts from" (T. S. Eliot) and "the place where when you have to go there, they have to take you in." (Robert Frost). A youngster growing up in a biological family, even the one who wishes that he or she could "turn in" the present parents and get new ones, assumes that the biological bond of the family is irrevocable. Only in imagination's realm can one find out that one was born to others. But this is one area in which it is difficult for an adopted child to behave like an ordinary kid. Adoptees are not likely to take their family bonds for granted.

Adoption originates in a social contract, and even the young adoptee intuitively understands that such a bond can be broken. "I was thrown to the wolves once!"

exclaimed adoptee Chuck Browne as he spoke to a group of parents of teenage adoptees. In his late twenties, Chuck was a trained social worker with a special interest in the problems of children. He told his listeners that it is hard for an adopted adolescent to feel secure enough to engage in the traditional rebellion against parental authority. "A person may not think in so many words, 'I was given away once, why couldn't it happen again?' But the feeling is always there." Chuck asked the group not to take his emotional statement about wolves too seriously, because like most adoptees, he had found the love and support he needed from his adoptive family. But, he explained, "Being adopted makes wanting to be on your own, to do your own thing, seem riskier."

A casual observer would not guess that the tall and handsome Chuck ever had concerns abut the value of his self. He seemed to have so much going for him. His intelligence and all-American blond good looks were part of his birth inheritance. His self-possessed manner, high achievements in school and career, and determination to excel at karate (he was a regional champion) owed much to his adoptive heritage.

Chuck continued, "Looking back on my life, I would say that I always felt that I arrived like an alien from an outer planet. When I was old enough to understand, I wondered a lot about my birth parents, especially who my father was and what he was like. I imagined that he was a boxer, or maybe a sailor—anyway, very different from my adoptive father, who's an insurance executive. My adoptive parents have always been there for me. I know there's a lot of love between us. But, after all, I was conceived and grew in another's womb. I was adopted at birth, but a child needs to be part of a real family even before being born." Chuck emphasized his point. "Know what I mean? To be wanted by the one giving birth. Obviously, I wasn't wanted by my birth parents the way I will want my own child some day."

Chuck hesitated a moment. "I felt I was forced to be on my own at the beginning of my life. I had no real connection to a human being, no person to think lovingly of me while I was still forming in the womb. Doctors, nurses, a lawyer, and a social worker attended the pregnant lady who was my birth mother, but there was no Mother for me, not then—not in the sense of having a real mother. When I was little, my parents told me the usual things about why I was adopted, and they were probably true: My birth parents were 'too young' and they 'wanted their child to have a good home.' When I was a young kid, that was fine. But when I got older, it horrified me to think of how my mother and father gave me away. Those feelings are there to rise up in you when you think your adoptive family might not approve of something you want to do." He grinned suddenly. "Let me tell you a little story.

"It was just after Christmas in my last year of high school. I had decided to use the money I was given by my grandparents to get a tattoo. All my friends were doing it, and the guy they went to was really an artist. When I mentioned the idea to my parents, they were dead set against it. Too 'lower-class,' they said. They were thinking about the old-time sailors, I guess. I don't believe they were thinking about my birth background, which was definitely lower class; I'm the one who made that connection.

"Anyway," Chuck continued, "after I saw their attitude, I didn't say any more to them about it. It was my body and my money. I just went ahead and got the tattoo, on my back just below my shoulder. They didn't know anything about it until Memorial Day, when we went on a family picnic the way we did every year. When I took my shirt off to go swimming, they saw it. My mother stared, but my father pretended he didn't see anything. He had to know what it was, though . . . it was a Norse symbol, and he's of Norwegian descent." Chuck explained that the tattoo—limited to one only, out of deference to his parent's feelings—represented an amulet that was supposed to protect the wearer on his journey into the next world. Then he added, "I told them, 'Aw, I only got it because it proves to the guys that I am your son.' "

Chuck had been successful in containing the contradictory pressures of adolescence that are often manifested in the so-called teen rebellion, without the excessive turmoil and extreme behavior of many teenagers. He reflected that he probably had spent too much time listening to rock music, hanging out with his friends, and driving around aimlessly after school, but he had avoided drugs and alcohol, and he was an excellent student. He and his parents usually got along fine. Indeed, they had in the end been reconciled to Chuck's tattoo, saying only, "We're glad you stopped at one." Chuck concluded, "They usually tried to see where I was coming from. I was sorry that they never said to me, 'Of course you are our son.' But I guess from their point of view, they didn't need to."

The young man mused aloud about his adolescent years, sharing his feelings with the group. "Maybe if we had talked more about certain things. . . . We did talk, actually, after I went to graduate school. I initiated the conversation. My parents were really surprised when I told them I had had a fantasy about being an alien. They had no idea I felt that way. I was worried that they might take what I said as some kind of criticism, but they didn't seem to. We still have a lot of talking to do. I tell my folks it's never too late!"

Chuck spoke briefly of the curiosity of the adoptee about the birth parents. Giving a short laugh, he said, "Of course I became curious when I hit my teens—and I still am." He drew an audible breath. "But I never wanted to search, even though I often thought about it. I don't think my folks would really mind, not now. But I could never bring myself to do more than think about it. To do it would take more courage than I'll probably ever have," said the muscular karate champ.

A Common Fantasy about Birth Parents

Youngsters who feel confidant about what they have and will have coming to them, can be comfortable with a variety of confrontational styles of communicating when they rebel. But the effect can be different for adoptees than for teenagers in a biological family. Helen, the mother of an adoptive son, recalled how she had once used the statement that she was adopted to assert herself within her own family. As a preteen, she was a fanatic reader of fairy tales and fantasies. Under the influence of one of her romantic books, Helen conceived the idea that she was born into a royal family but had been secretly spirited away by people of humble birth, who were charged with the task of raising and protecting her until she was old enough to come forth and claim her regal inheritance.

Helen's daydream was in some measure buttressed by the fact that she really was different from her parents, Eastern European immigrants to the land of opportunity. They called themselves by the negative label of "greenhorns," but took great pride in the fact that their daughter was a "real" American, native-born, instead of being naturalized, as they were. So in a way her parents actually supported her private fantasy of superior birth. When Helen went away to college, she was able to analyze that particular dynamic within her family, and let her rebellious fantasy go.

Discussing her youthful belief with her husband Bryan, Helen demonstrated how she had haughtily informed her long-suffering mother of her noble lineage. Throwing her head back in a gesture Bryan had never seen before, she dramatically declaimed, "I am of the Blood Royal! Perhaps I am even a Princess. I know it . . . I feel it." Bryan chuckled. He had never seen his modest and sensible wife like this before.

Even as a child, Helen was always aware that her adoption fantasy had no basis in reality. And she also knew that by expressing it so vocally, she hurt her mother's feelings. She had held on tenaciously, nevertheless, savoring a new and pleasing sense of power that substituted for her earlier docility. "I remember that I made Mother cry. I persisted in saying that I believed I was adopted, and I did want to believe that for quite a while," she added soberly.

It is likely that most parents would react with hurt and surprised anger to behavior like young Helen's, but it is also likely that most youngsters who would have such thoughts would considerately keep them to themselves. Despite her demureness, Helen had always had great curiosity, and that sometimes drove her into paths that discretion might have cautioned her against. In the beginning, she had mostly just wanted to know what her mother's reaction would be to her claim to be adopted; only afterwards did she begin to capitalize on it to gain her own ends. At her stage of life, Helen needed to be less involved with her parents, to move out into a greater degree of autonomy. As she discovered, her fantasy helped her accomplish this goal. By offending her parents, she was rewarded by their withdrawal. That allowed her to remove herself comfortably, without undue guilt, from the family embrace that had become too intensely enveloping.

The very term "adopted" has metaphorical significance within our culture. The adoptee is "gutsy" and "self-reliant," as symbolized by such folk heroes as Clark Kent and Little Orphan Annie. Or the adoptee is "pathetic," a cross between a servant and a companion to the adoptive family, like Charles Dickens' Tattycoram, or an abused scapegoat, like the Ugly Duckling of Hans Christian Andersen.

To those who are actually adopted, the term has a special reverberation. The adoptee is just as quick as anyone else to idealize, to pity, and to identify with the adoptees of myth and literature. However, unlike Helen and others who live in their biological families and therefore never run a real risk of confusing metaphor with reality, the adopted youngster may need help to separate the two. For adoptees, the dividing line between the real world and the world of imagination is not as well marked. The adoptive situation itself creates the problem. Contrast the story of Helen with that of her adopted son, Matty.

At twelve, Matty was a supremely confident young-ster, who seemed to have few doubts about his place in the world. One evening after dinner, Matty, Helen, and Bryan went out for a walk together. Matty was taking the family dog out for his nightly stroll, and his parents were on their way to a club meeting. Suddenly, empha-sizing each word, Matty stopped them in their tracks with his challenge.

"I do not believe what you told me about my birth parents. I believe that I am the son of GREAT people." His claim was unrealistic, for Helen and Bryan had certainly told the truth as they knew it when they ex-plained to Matty that his birth parents had been too young to make a good home for him. Matty understood the reality of his birth heritage, but it seemed that his primary intention was to irritate, perhaps even humili-ate, his parents.

Home again later that evening, with Matty in bed, Bryan revealed how disappointed he felt. "Could he really think we were lying to him about his birth par-ents?" Helen felt less troubled. She reminded her hus-band about her own youthful claim to adoptive status and a royal heritage. She speculated that Matty might already be entering his period of rebellion, and had chosen his adoptive status as an effective weapon to separate himself from his loving parents.

Helen convinced Bryan that Matty was simply using the idea of his birth parents as a strategy to achieve a measure of distance from them. Matty's action, of course, might also have been a cover for a deeper feeling of insecurity related to his having been given away, but if so, it was hidden; he seemed a model of self-confidence. Tactfully, Helen and Bryan did not openly reject their son's claim to be born of great people, even if they were hurt by his accusation that they had lied to him. They gave him the distance he craved, along with the opportunity to flex the muscles of his ego, as it were, and enjoy his emotional victory over them.

Accepting as they were of Matty's motivations, his parents nevertheless remained concerned about what the content of his confrontation might signify. Could it indicate that he had not come to realistic terms with his lack of meaningful knowledge about his birth family? They waited a few weeks, then raised the issue with their son again. The passage of time had helped them. They were able to discuss the subject in a calm and unruffled way. Matter of factly, and without making any connection between their present conversation and Matty's previous confrontation, Bryan pointed out that Matty was now old enough that he could, if he wished, discuss the circumstances of his adoption and check out the facts with a social worker at his adoption agency. He could even do it privately, alone with the social worker, and ask anything he wanted to know about. Matty's adoption agency made a practice of granting such an information-gathering interview to young adoptees, provided the adoptive parents gave their consent. Of course, names and addresses of the birth parents would not be revealed, but many details of the birth family history could be shared.

Matty liked his father's suggestion. At the age of twelve, being taken seriously is always gratifying. But, as it turned out, he was not motivated to follow through, and there the matter rested. Despite his bravado, Matty would have needed strong support from his parents had he decided to inquire into the reality of his birth family heritage. Many adoptees who have had the experience of talking to an adoption agency worker about information contained in their records report that it can be a devastating emotional experience, even when the worker is highly empathetic and the information available contains little that is strongly negative. The adoptee goes into the meeting with a welter of conflicts. There is the Need to be thoroughly informed about the birth identity; the Wish to know about the positive qualities associated with the birth family so they can be added with pride to the heritage of the adoptive family; and the Fear of learning facts that might be difficult to accept. A discussion with a stranger, no matter how understanding and sympathetic, is not enough to resolve all these issues. Matty probably didn't stop to analyze the situation in just this way, but at twelve, he was old enough to grasp intuitively that the experience could be overwhelming.

Embarrassment over the Adoptive Heritage

When Matty was fourteen, his attempts at adolescent rebellion took a more complicated turn. As he tried to integrate his birth heritage with the heritage of his adopted family, Matty once again drew on the fact that he had been adopted to hurt his parents and distance himself from them. This time it was the trans-racial aspect of his adoptive family that he used to make his points.

The previous year, his parents had enrolled him in a private junior high with an all-black student body. They had decided to take this step after anxiously watching their son's grades slip little by little over the previous three years in the integrated public school he attended.

Matty was an unusually bright youngster, and his academic achievement was important to his parents. They attributed his increasingly poor performance at school, and his growing indifference to academic matters, to a particular kind of inadequacy in his teachers. Helen thought the school took it for granted that youngsters of a minority race should not be expected to do as well as white children. "Not that his teachers weren't nice," Helen added. "They just didn't expect enough of black and Hispanic students, and Matty took advantage of the situation. Nothing we said to him seemed to make a difference." A note of exasperation crept into Helen's voice.

Matty rose to the challenge in his new school. He did so well that he was accepted into a city-wide honor high school. But when it came time for his graduation from private school, Matty informed his parents they would not be welcome at the ceremony. Stunned, they pressed him for an explanation. Finally, their son told them he was embarrassed that they were white.

Bryan and Helen could not hide their chagrin. They considered themselves a thoroughly integrated family. They had always lived in a multi-racial neighborhood and had close friends in the black community of their city. They cared about the destiny of blacks as well as whites. Indeed, they thought of themselves as "biracial." As was his wont, Bryan answered for his wife as well as himself. He tried to sound both reasonable and firm as he said, "Then you'll just have to be embarrassed." Retorted Matty, "If you come, I'll introduce you as my baby sitters." Stung, his father nevertheless remained outwardly calm as he replied, "Then I'll be contradicting you."

Before the big event, Bryan and Helen had a little talk with Matty. Privately, the couple had discussed together, in a kind of rehearsal, what they wanted to get across to their son. Their main point, they decided, was that in all things, the family was together; they were truly joined "for better or for worse." As the conversation they had rehearsed took place, Bryan added spontaneously, "We are mighty proud of you, Matty, and proud of ourselves as your parents. Let's talk some more about it later."

At the graduation ceremonies Matty was awarded a prize. Afterward, he introduced his parents to his classmates and their parents, and to his teachers. At home that evening, he commented, "It wasn't a piece of cake, you know."

"We know, we know," his parents chorused. "But we're so glad that you could do it."

Matty began his period of breaking away relatively early, and by the same token he seemed to finish early with his struggle to achieve the emotional distance he needed from his parents. Helen and Bryan, on the whole, handled this period wisely, informed in part by Helen's memory of her own need to break away from her parents. They did not retaliate when Matty took swipes at them, or attempted to manipulate them by using the family racial differences. Instead, they offered Matty a powerful lesson by behaving calmly and continuing to communicate their underlying love for their son, if not for his behavior. By their insistence that he could do more for himself, expressed in gestures such as offering him the opportunity to visit his social agency and enrolling him in a school that would offer him more of a challenge, they helped Matty in a practical way do more with his thinking self. The potential he had inherited from his birth parents. In helping him to fulfill his inherited potential, his parents had reconfirmed his adoptive heritage.

An Interest in Justice Can Provide Emotional Distance

Thoughts of right and wrong are a preoccupation of all ages of humankind. Youngsters in grade school and adolescents in high school have a special inclination towards philosophical reflections. Adopted youngsters are aware of the practical workings of justice as soon as they understand how society, in the form of the adoption process itself, has intervened in their own fate and the decision of their birth parents to give them away. Bart, a fourteen-year-old who had been born to a young girl unable to look after him, was adopted by Bella and Alfred before he was one year old. He used his inclination toward philosophical pondering to aid him in reaching the emotional distance he had begun to need from his adoptive mother.

One afternoon after school, Bart waited for his mother to pick him up. She was coming from a shopping trip downtown, and her way home would lie near his school. They took a route that swung through an older section of the city, where the family had lived when Bart was an infant. Stopping for a red light, Bella noticed the nursery school her son had attended. Nostalgically pointing it out, she instinctively reached over and grabbed her son's hand. "There is your old playground," she cooed. Bart jerked his hand away from hers and yelled, "Watch out! Watch out! You'll have an accident!" But the light was still red, and the car was not moving.

As Bella glanced curiously at Bart, he abruptly changed the subject. He asked, "Who should I love more, you or my birth mother?"

Bella, suddenly very flustered, wanted to answer her son's question in a reasonable manner, so she took her time to find the right words. "Love is not something you measure like flour or sugar. It is something you can feel for both of us." Her logical, yet still idealistic, answer seemed to satisfy Bart, and he turned to more mundane interests. Bella chose not to respond to the subtext of her son's message, at least not in so many words. Later, when she noticed that she no longer felt free to be so openly affectionate toward him, she recognized that her behavior began to change from that moment in the car when he pulled his hand away from hers and shouted about the nonexistent accident. She realized that "he forced me to see that he was growing up, and that a display of maternal affection made him embarrassed and uneasy."

Bart was still too young to give much thought to broad social issues, such as the plight of women who have babies out of wedlock, and it is doubtful that he was truly motivated by an ethical point of view when he brought up the subject of love in regard to his birth mother. Probably he used the idea primarily to assist himself in his adolescent struggle to let go of his adoptive mother. Mentioning a second mother put the first one in her proper place, or so it would seem. Bella's answer, however, communicated both information and comfort. It signalled her acceptance of his desire for distance at the same time that it taught him something important: that an ethical concern about his birth mother was not in reality amiss. An adoptee who can identify sympathetically with problems faced by birth parents and find the parents worthy has better feelings about the self than the adoptee who must reject the birth parents entirely.

Memories of the Birth Parents

A happy present appears to change the unhappy past. That is fortunate for the youngster adopted when older, who comes with conscious memories of the birth family history that must be integrated into the adoptee's dual identity. Terri, whose olive skin, brown eyes, and curly brown hair revealed her Hispanic background, was the oldest of three girls born to a drug-addicted mother. Terri was so seriously neglected by her birth mother that the Children's Court removed the little girl from her mother's custody when she was three and placed her in a foster home. Terri made a good adjustment to the change. Her physical health improved, and she developed a sense of trust in the foster parents who cared for her. Her birth mother never visited her, nor showed any signs of interest in the girl.

After the legally required period had elapsed, Terri was declared adoptable. At four and a half, she was adopted by Gloria and Tony Manetti. Again, the little girl made a good adjustment to the major changes in her life, becoming attached not only to her adoptive parents but also to her new brother, Ralph, her parents' biological son.

Terri did not talk about her birth mother until after she entered school. Then she began to express curiosity about her mother's present life. It was apparent that she had some actual memory of her birth mother, not just a confusion with her foster mother. Gloria, who knew many details of the history of Terri's birth family, was greatly surprised to hear that the child's memories of her birth mother were rosy.

How can we understand the apparent selectivity of Terri's memory? A 1987 study (as reported in *The New York Times,* June 23, 1987) demonstrated that unwanted chapters of earlier personal history were typically wiped out of the memory of adults whose unhappy childhood lives had subsequently improved. Another study confirms that children with an early experience of physical and emotional deprivation "forgot" their unhappy past when they made good adjustments to adoption (Kadushin, 1970). This healing process of "forgetting" might be stated another way: as an example of the workings of the ubiquitous Good Mother fantasy. Remember, even a generally bad mother is not bad all the time; there are certainly some good moments, however rare. When Terri let her imagination claim her birth mother as the Good Mother, she eliminated the reality of her birth mother's neglect.

Like other children her age, Terri was deeply moral. In her eyes, the doctrine of fairness was primary. Not only curious about her birth mother, she was now becoming concerned about her welfare. When the day to honor all mothers was approaching, Terri asked her adoptive mother if she should not send a Mother's Day card to her birth mother. Gloria privately thought her daughter had no need to feel obligated. Nevertheless, she did her best to try to see the situation from the little girl's point of view. Terri felt she should treat her birth mother just as well as she treated her adoptive mother. Unlike Bart, who used the idea of the birth mother as a kind of tool to achieve some distance from his adoptive mother, Terri was chiefly concerned about doing the right thing by a person she actually remembered, if only in a distorted way. The earliest memories of life are often not visual and are extremely difficult to put into words. This makes them particularly susceptible to subsequent distortion.

Terri expressed her notion of fair play succinctly: "I give *you* a card, Mom." Gloria handled the situation by asking her daughter what she would most *want* to do. Through this message, she gave her daughter an alternate way to look at the situation, other than only as a matter of conscience. Terri responded to this new viewpoint by saying in a mildly worried way that she did not know what she really wanted to do. Gloria said reassuringly, "If you really want to send a card, it certainly would be right." She added that she would help by getting the birth mother's address. On the other hand, Gloria continued, if Terri did not want to send a card, and only thought she *should*, she need not. That would be alright, too. By suggesting these choices, Gloria encouraged Terri to think about her own needs more objectively.

Terri did decide she wanted to send her birth mother a card. Gloria kept her promise and located the birth mother's address. No acknowledgement of the card ever came. Gloria comforted Terri by sharing her daughter's disappointment. Then she added that the silence of Terri's birth mother did not necessarily mean she didn't care about Terri. Gloria reminded Terri that her birth mother "had very serious problems" which were the reason Terri had originally been sent to a foster home. Being "disorganized," as Gloria characterized the birth mother's behavior, was close to, if not the entire truth of the matter, and Gloria's positive perspective helped protect Terri's sense of self-worth.

Were Terri to have become convinced that her birth mother was bad, it would have increased the girl's vulnerability to the Bad Seed fantasy. Yet the Manettis' values and behavior were deeply at odds with those of Terri's birth mother. Whatever their most private thoughts, they were able to avoid speaking harshly of her by following certain communication guidelines. They recognized and respected Terri's emotional needs. And they made an effort to use terminology that conveyed the facts about Terri's birth heritage in a non-judgmental way.

The Struggle to Grow Roots

Despite her disappointment, Terri seemed to be comfortable in her dual attachments. She continued to speak of her birth mother favorably and soon began to wonder what her half-sisters were like, deciding they must be "cute." Yet all the while, she was undergoing an inner struggle of which her parents were unaware. Insight came with a surprising event that revolved around her brother Ralph.

The following autumn, just after school reopened, Ralph fell severely ill while studying in his Home Room. He was rushed to the emergency room of the nearest hospital. At first the examining physicians thought the boy had suffered a seizure, but they later determined his condition was the result of a severe allergic reaction to fumes that were drifting past his seat from an alcove that was being repainted. In the course of establishing this diagnosis, it was unexpectedly discovered that

Ralph had an unrecognized genetic problem, *Thalasse-mia minor*. It is a silent condition often called "the Mediterranean trait" because it is commonly found among people with a Mediterranean heritage. Its gravity lies entirely in the fact that when both parents carry the gene, children are at risk for the life-threatening disease, *Thalassemia major*. Therefore the doctors treating Ralph requested that the rest of the family also be tested for the gene, so they could get a better picture of the way the trait was distributed and alert the family to possible future risk. Gloria and Tony, both from Italian back-grounds, decided to include Terri in the tests, so she would not feel left out, or different from her adoptive family. Sharing bad times as well as good is important to establishing roots.

When the physicians informed the family of the test results, Gloria and Tony were surprised to learn that not only was Tony a carrier, so was Terri. Apparently she too had a Mediterranean birth heritage. They felt deep sor-row for their adopted daughter's sake. This was a piece of bad luck for a child who had already had more than her share. But Terri was completely undismayed. Perhaps she was too young to understand fully what the news might mean to her in the future. For the present, though, her thoughts were entirely occupied with the new simi-larity she shared with her father and brother. "I am glad, glad, glad!" Tony and Gloria were shocked to hear their daughter say. She seemed almost to be dancing even though seated in a plastic chair in the doctors' office. "Now I have something just like Daddy and Ralph. Now I really belong!"

Driving home from the hospital, the family reflected on life's unexpected twists and turns. Ralph, sitting in the front seat, turned around to look at his sister and started to say something. Gloria, sitting next to her daughter, picked up a hesitation in the boy's manner. She thought she knew what he wanted to say, so she helped him out. Putting her arms around Terri's shoulders, she emphasized, "You are one of us and there is no doubt about it. You don't need the trait to prove it!" Tony nodded to show his agreement, and then swung the car into a parking spot in front of their favorite coffee shop. It was time to lighten up the afternoon.

Although the subject was closed for that day, the issue of belonging, with its roots in the dual nature of an adoptee's heritage, was probably never far below the surface for Terri. Her feelings about it were influenced by the fact that she had memories of belonging to another family. The memories would sometimes interfere with her present happiness. For example, when good things happened in her life, she would wonder with a sense of guilt over her better fortune about her half-sisters and whether they were alright. She might always long to hear from her birth mother and feel anger and sadness that she did not. Yet how could she make a decision to forget all her past? She could not reasonably be expected to destroy all her memories at will. She would always feel a pull toward her birth heritage.

It was different for the Manettis. They had made a conscious choice to adopt an older child, and they were happy with the way things were turning out. They had no feelings of ambivalence about Terri. From their point of view, she belonged to their family without question. It was because the Manettis could feel that way, yet understand that Terri's feelings were more ambivalent, that the girl was able to settle into the family and eventually feel entitled to all they had to give.

The Vulnerability of the Trans-racially Adopted Child

Many minority youngsters adopted by white parents face the issues of their adolescence and earlier school years in an especially vulnerable position. By adolescence, often even earlier, they have become aware of the lower status forced by society on minority races and of a resulting personal stigma. Even if the adoptive family is entirely successful in coping with all the differences within the family itself, no parent can completely protect a trans-racially adopted child from the pain caused by racial slurs from outsiders. And children are not always ready to talk out their disturbing thoughts and feelings about the situation, even in families where frank talk is the norm. A child may have the need for privacy, may want to maintain an inner life without the intrusion of others, no matter how well-intentioned.

Parents of a trans-racially adopted child have a particular anxiety when their child reacts negatively but the cause of the reaction is not obvious. Is the problem one that is characteristic of all children? Or of all adoptees? Or is it more specifically an issue of trans-racial adoption? Parents often must rely on their intuitive knowledge of their own child, because there may be no overt signs to follow.

Betty Marks was black, adopted into a family (including an older brother, Martin) that was white. Dark-skinned Betty had been born of a white birth mother who had had an affair with a much older black man. Little besides that was known of the girl's birth heritage.

When Betty was eight, the family spent a summer vacation month in the country. They had rented a cozy cottage on a lake. They were all happy with the location: the warm lake to swim in and the little bit of sandy beach where the children could play, the piney woods behind the cottage with interesting sites to explore. The only drawback was that there were no black families among the summer residents, and only white children for Betty, accustomed to an integrated environment, to play with.

One Sunday they decided to go to the County Fair. Betty's one friend, a girl her age named Sally, was away on a picnic with her family and so Betty had no companion of her own. Once in the milling crowd, the girl clung to her mother, pulling her arm back so tightly that it was painful. She seemed to be trying to hide behind her mother's body. "What's the matter?" Claire questioned. Betty gave no answer. But she did loosen her grip a little bit, while still clutching her mother's hand.

At home that evening, Claire interrupted Betty as she sat watching television after dinner. She was only guessing when she asked her daughter, "Did it bother you to go where there are just white people?" Her straightforward question was answered with equal candor. "Yes," said Betty, "it did." Claire then made a revelation that surprised Betty: She too had been bothered by the situation. Betty had not thought of that point of view, and the idea intrigued her. They began to talk about the differences among people, and Claire asked, "Do you know why people are different all over the world?" Betty answered yes, it was because of "evolution." Then her mother asked her why she thought so many people get uncomfortable and act mean about differences. Betty did not have an answer for that question. Her mother explained that some people need to see that everybody else is just like themselves. Otherwise, they feel that something is "wrong" with them.

It was growing late. Betty said goodnight and went to her room to get ready for bed. The following week, the family returned to their home in the city. All seemed well. But, that November, a more obvious incident of prejudice occurred. The Marks family was visiting white friends, spending the day at their comfortable home in an all-white suburb. Betty walked into the dining room moodily, dragging her feet as she often did when she was feeling unhappy. She announced in dejected tones, "A boy called me 'nigger'." Claire lost her temper over the insult to her daughter. She put down her fork and emphasized each separate word. "In that case, the next time you see him I give you my permission to punch him in the nose." Betty answered seriously that she would not be able to do that because the boy was too big. Her older brother Martin, who had overheard the conversation from the other end of the dining table, tried to help. He said. "That boy is ignorant, Bets. He's probably never been more than ten miles from this place." Her family's response was well-meant, and surely their words communicated the comfort of their love, even if the message lacked any real informational content.

As Betty grew older, the focus of her painful reaction to such overt racial slurs, and more subtle stigmatization, did not so much shift as grow more inclusive and more intense. On another occasion, not much later in time, she brought up the subject of her (white) birth mother. "She wouldn't have a reason to see me," she said to her adoptive mother in a dreary voice. "She probably has a white family now." It seemed that as Betty became more aware of the complexities of her own dual heritage as an adoptee, her relationship to her birth mother—fantasized but based on the reality that she had been given away by a white woman—was becoming more painful.

One day in her fifteenth year, Betty and her mother were together in the family car. It was early Sunday afternoon, and they were moving along at low speed through a black middle class neighborhood, looking for the house of a girl from Betty's school who was having a birthday party. Unfortunately, without pausing to reflect on her words, Claire suddenly asked her daughter if she would prefer to live in a black neighborhood like this one, instead of their own integrated neighborhood. She had been thinking to herself only that such a situation might be comfortable for Betty, but her daughter's reply ran contrary to her expectations. Betty said no most emphatically, adding, "I would have to live in a ghetto with the door of my tenement swinging wide open to the hall."

The message Claire intended to send her daughter was, Wouldn't it be nice if we all lived here together, sharing your heritage. Betty, however, heard a different message. She interpreted her mother's remark, admittedly not very carefully phrased, as meaning that as a black person she was not "good enough"—not good enough to live with her white adoptive family.

In adolescence, competitive issues are important. An adolescent girl must feel comfortable in competing within the family, and most particularly in competing with her own mother in regard to issues like, "Am I the most beautiful?" Her answer, to herself, must be yes.

When a girl develops normally, she need feel neither anger over her frustration that she can't always win, nor guilt over the fact that she is competing. If she is to be successfully motivated to become a winner in the life that lies ahead, she needs to feel emotionally entitled by her mother to shine in her turn, even if that does put the older woman a bit in the shade.

Betty, although black, had in earlier years succeeded in identifying herself with Claire, and had become like Claire in her basic attitudes toward life. Yet she did not deny her blackness, in the manner of some trans-racially adopted children, out of respect for her own racial individuality. Her ability to feel comfortably different from the rest of the family was part of the heritage her adoptive parents had given her. Yet, having kept her black identity, in adolescence she could not help but be deeply aware of the position of the black race in society in general, and to feel deeply marked by it, even in regard to her relationship with her adoptive mother. It made the competitive feelings toward the older woman that were quite normal for her age subtly threatening and painful, no matter how hard her mother tried to make her feel comfortable about them. In her burgeoning competitiveness, Betty did not even *fantasize* a benign situation in which she could compete safely with her white mother. She would have to live in a ghetto, the door to the hall swinging open.

The onus of helping adoptees with problems that are caused by the existence of birth parents, who are often unknown or mysterious, falls on the adoptive parents. In Betty's case, it was up to Claire especially; the youngster needs most of all the encouragement of the parent of the same sex. It would take a number of years and many painful experiences—including the pain that she would inflict on her adoptive family, for in time she became a runaway—before Betty could settle within herself all that she felt her unasked-for destiny had heaped upon her.

But neither Betty nor her adoptive mother suspected all that lay ahead before Betty's struggle was won, that afternoon in the family car. Her mother simply disagreed with Betty's comment about having to live in a ghetto, in a reassuring communication. "No, dear, you would not live in a bad place. You would not, because you would make a different kind of life for yourself." Claire thus stressed her message that she believed Betty would be able to face the future in a positive manner. This kind of communication, at once comforting and informative, was the foundation that Betty could build on. Far off in the future, it would help to bring her back to her adoptive home and to a resumption of the life she threw aside for a time.

8 Looking to the Future

In the eyes of a little boy, his father is always a hero. The boy is filled with admiration, and the wish to emulate. In the so-called Oedipal phase of child development, he even claims that he wants to marry his own mother when he grows up. The mythological story of Oedipus, as told by the Greek dramatist Sophocles, concerns an infant son, who adopted and deprived of birth family information, grows up to slay his birth father and take his birth mother's hand in marriage, all unwittingly. Freud was inspired to name the childhood period in which competitiveness arises in a child toward the parent of the same sex after this tragic hero.

As a boy grows, the importance of such feelings recedes, subdued by the clamor of new interests. Eventually, the boy will emerge from his adolescence with the convictions of an adult, that he knows where he is going and what he wants. Yet, what his father is and has been always strongly influences the son. The folk wisdom contained in such adages as "Like father, like son," or "The fruit never falls far from the tree" points out this universal truth.

Yet it is difficult for the teenaged boy to recognize how persuasive a model his father is, during the period when he is doing his best to establish his independence of the older man. (During the boy's period of teenaged rebellion, it may also be difficult for the father to remember that truth as well.) The typical rebellious adolescent boy would probably deny that he wants to become like his father and that he will want to find a wife like his father's choice—that is, like his mother. He does not recognize that his wishes for his own future achievements, his hopes of winning admiration, are grounded in what he has all along found good and worthwhile in his father.

Nor is the teenager aware that alongside his love and admiration, indeed rooted in it, are other, more aggressive (although not necessarily hostile) feelings. "Yes," the boy might acknowledge freely, he wouldn't mind being "even better" at something than his old man, but chances are he would not perceive the aggression concealed within the wish. For that matter, his father may have similarly aggressive feelings, and they may be similarly well hidden. Sometimes, of course, the feelings of aggression are not hidden at all, and father and teenaged son clash openly.

The growing girl goes through a similar process. In her Oedipal period, her competitiveness develops and emerges to jostle her love and admiration for her mother. She would like to marry her father, her mother's man, when she grows up. Later, she too will give up on the intensity of her love for her father and her original competitive goal, as in adolescence she becomes immersed in new interests that will carry her beyond her parents' family and out into her own life as an adult.

Gratitude

The adolescent process of challenging and competing with parents is especially complicated for adoptees. An adopted teenager's feelings of gratitude for the very fact of being adopted, for having a family and home, make for a special pressure. All adolescents, whether living in a biological or an adoptive family, do of course share in that particular sense of connectedness to parents that is a child's gratitude. It is as old as a child's very self, seen in the smile, so suffused with pleasure, that an infant gives Mother in response to her good nurturance and her loving playfulness. As an adolescent, the adopted child is able to comprehend how much life has differed in its quality because of the fact that an adoption took place. The result is that the teenager may feel that sense of filial gratitude to such a degree that it becomes tinged with an uncomfortable sense of guilt.

A sense of guilt is especially likely to surface on those occasions when the youngster believes that he or she might appear ungrateful. A teenager might define as an ungrateful act one that is entirely symbolic. For example, a boy who beats his father in a chess game, or a girl who enjoys compliments that imply she is prettier than her mother might convict themselves of ingratitude. Yet winning, or doing better than a parent, is not usually something that the parent minds. Father has been coaching his son for years so the boy will be able to beat him at chess; Mother remembers enjoying her own flush of beauty as a young woman, and vicariously shares her daughter's pleasure. It is actually a goal for many parents to see their children's achievements exceed their own. It may be hard for adoptees to recognize that altruistic desire in their parents, and to understand that parents want to share the rewards of being grown up with their almost grown-up child. Their parents' acceptance may seem to be just one more reason to feel grateful—and guilty—no matter how thoroughly independent they have been brought up to be.

This complicated emotional mix of gratitude and guilt is not necessarily easy for either parents or teenagers to recognize. It creates so much discomfort that a young adoptee will ignore it, disguise its meaning, put it out of sight, keep it out of mind. It may make it more difficult for an adoptee to strike out on his or her own when the time comes. Such mixed feelings sometimes crystallize into a fear of success. That is, the adoptee avoids success, fearful that any achievement will somehow actually hurt a parent. Parents who are aware of their child's discomfort about these feelings are better able to help them let it go.

Fathers and Sons

Fourteen-year-old Deke Mandell could not have explained his feelings that day in August, when he and his father were driving from their home in suburban Westchester County to the stadium in Forest Hills, where they had good seats for the U.S. Open tennis matches. In fact, his feelings were no more clear to him than they were to be to his father, when Deke tried to speak of his concerns.

The silence between father and son was a companionable one. Henry, an opera buff, was humming a comic aria from "The Barber of Seville" as he drove. Deke was mulling over the coming school year. He would be starting his first semester of high school in a few weeks, and he had yet to decide what foreign language to take. Should he opt for Spanish or German? Spanish might be good for a business career in New York, with its large Hispanic population; German is the traditional choice for a career in science or medicine.

When he was younger, Deke had found it easier to make decisions. At five, he "knew" that he would be either a policeman or a fireman when he grew up. At eight, he confidently thought he would like to be an executive, like his father. Now that the future was drawing closer, he was no longer so sure of his preferences. But he comforted himself with the thought that if he picked the "wrong" language now, he could always study the "right" one later, in college or graduate school. He knew his parents were fully committed to giving him all the education he desired.

Deke was a full-blooded American Indian, adopted at the age of one by Henry and his wife Rosemary. As the little boy grew up, friends and relatives all exclaimed over the "amazing" resemblance between Deke and his adoptive father. In actual fact, not a single one of their facial features was similar. But out of love and admiration for his father, Deke gradually took on more and more of Henry's mannerisms. He walked heavily on his heels, just like his dad. He wrinkled up his nose the same way when he laughed. He squinted his right eye when he was being serious, and that was like his dad too. Deke even had the high-pitched laugh, nearly a giggle, that Henry had inherited from his own father.

The silence in the car was finally broken by Deke, when they were still at some distance from the stadium. His simple statement was so quietly uttered that it almost escaped his father's attention, which was fixed on the worsening traffic (and the comic aria he was humming.) Deke said, "Dad, I feel FUNNY that I don't know what my birth father does."

Henry stopped humming. "What?" he asked in astonishment. Deke repeated his words.

It was not surprising that Deke did not know what his birth father did for a living; adoptees typically do not possess that kind of information about their birth families. But why would Deke think of this question now? What connection did his birth father have to Deke's life at this moment of the here and now?

Watching the road signs carefully, Deke's father spoke with a ringing note of conviction in his voice. "You are not a 'funny' kid, Deke. Believe me, you are a winner." Then, eyes still glued to the road, he added, "It's the situation that's funny, not you. You know what I mean?" Deke did know what his father meant; how could he not? They had talked about the complexities of the adoptive situation many times before. His father had often expressed his strong belief that it was an adoptee's right to have any available information about his birth family. Deke was glad his father felt that way, for it gave him a good feeling of acceptance of himself. When parents defend the denial of information that is so often the policy of adoption agencies, adolescents often interpret their attitude as meaning, "The facts about my birth family must be so bad that they have to be kept a secret from me."

Henry's response to his son's comment was based on his conclusion that Deke was talking about the stigma of adoption, which made him feel that he was "funny" in comparison to other teens. But Deke's parents had for years given him a great deal of emotional support about the problems he faced living by social rules that are different than they are for children raised in their biological families. Because his parents had always been so supportive, Deke didn't really need to be reassured about his value as a human being, nor about adoptive issues in general. His father's good intentions had led to a misinterpretation of Deke's remark. Bringing up the subject of his birth father was a signal that there was something else on Deke's mind.

Had his father realized what was really on Deke's mind, he could have helped him then and there continue along that line of thought (or imagination). With the new viewpoint of adolescence, Deke was thinking about fathers and sons. There was the mystery of his relationship with his unknown birth father, and the reality of his relationship with his adoptive father. But Deke could not continue to discuss his thoughts or feelings about the subject of fathers and sons without some help and guidance, for he did not know how. An inchoate train of thought, a wish largely unformulated, is not easy to explain.

An example taken from an earlier period of Deke's life demonstrates how hard it can be for a child to communicate what he is really thinking, and how much a parent can do to facilitate the process. This little story has two morals that apply to all family communication, no matter what the age of the child. One is that words are variable in their meaning; the speaker who uses them may intend one meaning, while the listener interprets them to mean something quite different. The second moral of Deke's story is that a child not only wants but expects a magical understanding from his parents, no matter how hidden his message may be.

When Deke was about sixteen months old, his parents took him to visit his adoptive mother's cousins, who had a summer cottage fronting a lake in the White Mountains of New Hampshire. The long narrow lot on which the house was built ran up the hill behind it; at the very top was an old tennis court, fallen into disrepair. Henry, even then a tennis enthusiast, had been curious about the court, and started off along the narrow footpath, nearly hidden by green overgrowth, to take a look. His son toddled unsteadily after him. As they walked along, the child's hand securely held in his father's, Deke looked with interest at the tall grasses, the same height as he was, among which were a few ragged daisies and some dandelions and buttercups.

"See!" Deke pointed. "See!" He tugged on his father's hand. "Yes, I do see," said Henry, assuming that Deke was telling him to look at the wild flowers along the path. They walked a few steps more, and Deke again tugged at his father's hand and repeated his urgent message: "See!" Henry made the same reply, this time giving the flowers a closer look to show that he was following the boy's instruction. This little scene was repeated every few steps. Deke seemed inexhaustible, and Henry was beginning to find his son's constantly repeated urging tiresome. He tried to pick Deke up and carry him the rest of the way to the tennis court, but the boy protested loudly. He wanted to walk himself—and he wanted to continue telling his father to "See!"

Fortunately, the light finally dawned on Henry. As he later explained to his wife, he did at last "see." He understood that Deke was using the word "see" to mean something different from Henry's interpretation. Deke was not asking Henry to look, but was asking him to understand that his son could see for himself: that he observed those wonderful green things he had never seen before, the delicate waving leaves along the overgrown footpath, the fat yellow buttercups and the low round dandelions. When Henry ultimately realized the message his son was trying to convey, he gave the boy a different answer. "Yes," he affirmed, "*you* do see, yes, yes, you do." Deke looked up at his father with a beatific smile, and Henry was happy to know that he had finally given the boy the confirmation he was looking for.

At fourteen, Deke had grown up to be one of the fortunate youngsters able to sustain the belief that they "have what it takes:" adequate intelligence, sufficient physical strength, ordinary good looks and doting parents eager to provide all else that is necessary. Deke took seriously his parents' adage, "You can be anything you want to be." He was not yet aware that this belief laid a tremendous responsibility on him, but he realized that he might well have more choices in life than either his adoptive father, who had worked tremendously hard to get where he was, or his birth father, who probably had very little in the way of material success.

Had father and son talked about the mystery of Deke's birth father's vocation, their conversation would inevitably have led to further hypotheses about the general circumstances of that unknown man's life. Then the talk could have turned to Deke's underlying sense of guilt that was mingled with his gratitude for his own good fortune, touching on how the boy felt about all that his adoptive parents had given him. His father might then have been able to follow up with some advice on how a fortunate young person can repay the gifts received from his elders. Deke might, for example, join a volunteer group to work for the environment or to help the homeless. He might later in life become a father, adoptive or otherwise, and pass along his good fortune to a new generation. A resolve to help others is a time-honored way to solve the problems of too much filial gratitude that can begin to produce guilt.

But Deke and his father did not have that conversation that day in the car. In this silence, they were probably typical. According to adoption research, it is the rare family that talks together about the deeper issues of adoptive relationships. Did it matter, in the long run, that the two didn't continue their talk that day? There is no way to know for sure. Yet the problem of too much (contaminated) gratitude can result in real problems if unchecked.

Henry's response was perhaps not the one most helpful to Deke at that very moment. As in the incident when Deke was a toddler, Henry misinterpreted the real message that his son was trying to communicate, and as a teenager, Deke was no longer so persistent. Yet even though Henry framed his answer with a different issue in mind than the one his son was thinking about, it was nevertheless helpful to Deke. It did convey Henry's wish to support his son emotionally, and in that way it was an invitation to the boy to continue to talk about what was on his mind. If that ever took place, though, it would have to be on another day. Deke had just caught sight of the stadium up ahead. His father would want his help in finding a good parking space. They were both already getting caught up in the excitement of the world-class matches about to start, an interest Deke had learned to share with Henry. Nothing else would be important to either son or father until they were in their seats, and then the games would begin.

Mothers and Daughters

"Being like you, Mom, that's what I really want." Sweet words—an adolescent daughter's thank you for her mother's loving care during all those years she was growing up. And being like her mother gives a daughter an important sense of direction that she needs, a kind of map to guide her along as she reaches toward independence and begins to think about finding her own career, and especially important in this context, looking for a life's partner with whom to establish a family of her own. Being like one's mother does not necessarily mean looking like her or having the same temperamental characteristics. It can mean simply an attitude about things. The similarity may be expressed in small ways, like making potato salad the same way, with pickles and without hard-boiled egg. Or it may be deeply rooted, for example, in the attitude that a mother should not work during the first several years of her child's life. Most girls learn how to be a good mother from the original model of their own mothers' nurturance.

All growing girls expect that their body will change outwardly and inwardly as they grow. Eventually, it will look and be like the body of an adult woman, like that of their mother. When she reaches her teen years, the adopted daughter of an infertile mother faces a distressing conflict.

Like most girls, fifteen-year-old Louise closely identified her image of her maturing body with the image of her mother's body. Because her parents had been direct in their conversations about adoptive issues over the years, Louise knew that they had turned to adoption because her mother was unable to bear a child of her own. Her apprehensions that she might be like her mother in this way were increased because she was late in starting to menstruate. Although her mother's infertility was not at all linked to menstrual problems, that was no reassurance to frightened Louise. She feared that she had been given a sign by fate that she too would be infertile.

The adopted girl's psychological development requires that she, like girls who live with their biological mothers, identify positively with her mother. Yet in that one regard, her adoptive mother's procreative failure, how can she? Louise struggled with the problem. The best solution, she later recognized, would have been to talk things out with her parents—especially her mother. But her mother, usually so supportive, could not talk about this issue, for she had not resolved her own deep sadness over her infertility. With the best will in the world, parents are not always able to give their child exactly what is needed. So there was never a family conversation that tried to reassure Louise that she would in all likelihood be fertile in the normal way, as most adoptees are; or explain that medical advances now permitted many infertile women to conceive; and, most important of all, to tell Louise that being an adoptive parent brings its own joys.

Louise dealt with her dilemma in the way many teen-aged adoptees do: She conjured up an image of her unknown birth mother to comfort herself. Although Louise had virtually no information about her birth mother, she knew there was one fact that was indisputable, her birth mother's fertility. Each adopted girl's way of building a picture of her birth mother is unique to her. Louise, who like most adoptees had no concrete facts to assist her in imagining her birth mother, started with her own physical appearance. She made the natural assumption that she bore a resemblance to her unknown birth mother. Louise was a classical type, although she had not yet had exposure to Greco-Roman culture and therefore did not realize how close she came to that ideal of beauty. Tall and slender, Louise tended to wear her thick honey-colored hair severely pulled back from her face, to show off the symmetry of her features. Her square jaw gave her a commanding look. Active in school dramatics, she found she was always given the authoritative roles in plays, such as queen or teacher. She had once even been asked to play the part of the Chinese emperor in a drama about Marco Polo. The dramatics coach had commented that none of the boys looked sufficiently regal; only Louise had the splendid look of one born to expect instant obedience.

So Louise started by imagining her birth mother as a tall slim woman with an air of self-possession. Then, when Louise was in her third year of high school, she found further material for building an image of her birth mother. In French class, her teacher showed a film about the Statue of Liberty, explaining how it had been a gift to America from the French people. The homework assignment for that day was to translate the English inscription on its base, written by Emma Lazarus, into French. It read:

> Give me your tired, your poor,
> Your huddled masses yearning to breathe free,
> The wretched refuse of your teeming shore,
> Send these, the homeless, tempest-tossed to me,
> I lift my lamp beside the golden door.

These moving words were especially significant to the adopted teenager, symbolizing for her a wise mother spirit. If only her birth mother were like the Statue, would want to see her again, undo the adoption, and take her in! The poem might even more accurately be interpreted to symbolize the open arms and welcoming heart of an adoptive mother, but Louise didn't need to create an image of her adopted mother, for she possessed the reality. Such is the power of the imagination, and the strength of Louise's need to identify with her birth mother's fertility, that she could wish her adoption undone, even though she loved her adoptive parents and never really seriously thought of not being their child.

Louise's imagination was helped along by a coincidence. There was a real resemblance between her own physical features and those of the famous icon. The teenager began to daydream that there might be a blood connection between herself and the model who posed for the statue. In that way, she partially convinced herself that she was a secret descendant of the mother of the sculptor, Frederic Bartholdi, for it was his mother who sat for him. Perhaps Madame Bartholdi was Louise's great-great-great grandmother—or at least that's what Louise fervently hoped. Surely, she reasoned, she was at least of French descent; she must have some genetic relationship to the woman she so resembled. Louise began to tell her friends she had reason to believe that she was of French background. But her common sense kept her from revealing what that reason was.

Eventually, Louise disclosed her belief to her parents. They did not try to dissuade her, knowing she would give it up in good time—when she could do without the reassurance. They recognized that she had a good grasp of the difference between what was real and what was only in her imagination. Sympathetic to their daughter's wish to have the kind of ancestral roots that only one's bloodline can confer, they expressed their agreement that Louise's features bore an astonishing resemblance to Miss Liberty.

But, because the family never spoke openly together about the issue of fertility, Louise's parents did not realize what it was that had sparked her quest for some sort of birth history and an identification with her birth mother: her fear that she might, like her adoptive mother, be infertile. That very fear was an important, although unrecognized, motive in her decision to marry soon after she graduated from college. Her parents were not wholeheartedly in favor of such an early marriage, fearing that Louise was too young and inexperienced to make a wise decision regarding marriage. As it turned out, their concern was well founded. Louise's marriage was of short duration. But it did last long enough for her to become a mother, finally allaying the fear of infertility that had so long been in the back of her mind.

As an adolescent, Louise did not perceive all the reasons she related so strongly to the statue that symbolizes a safe haven for the needy of the world. When she later became a pediatric nurse, she began to understand the power that symbol had held for her in her teens. She became aware that a need to emulate that all-giving maternal symbol was probably the basis of her career decision. (A keen interest in the issues of safety and rescue is characteristic of many adoptees.) When Louise looked back on her adolescence from an adult point of view, she regretted that she had never been able to talk to her parents about her half-understood fears. Had they themselves been able to confront the issue of infertility squarely, Louise might have been more able to differentiate between her own fate and that of her mother. Had her mother reassured her, she might have been able to see that she could be like her adoptive mother, without being exactly like her in every way. She might not have needed that special birth mother image (although the effects of her fantasy were largely benign). More important, she might not have needed to test her ability to become a mother herself, before she was fully ready. Yet she recognized how hard it was for her parents to talk about why they had decided to adopt, and knew that they had done their best. As an adult herself, she was aware that all adults have their limitations.

Comparisons

The strong feelings of teenagers sometimes do upset their own equilibrium as well as that of the rest of the family. One of the more difficult and perplexing feelings is the fear of failing to measure up to the parent of the same sex. This fear is not limited to biological children; many adopted adolescents must face it as well. Their way of coping with the feeling, however, can be different from that of the youngster raised in a biological family. The adoptee has avenues of expression closed to others, and adoptive parents need a nimble understanding to handle the situation.

Adopted at birth, Andy had grown into a handsome teenager. His parents, Wallace and Emma, were proud of his pleasant disposition and excellent grades in school. Andy and his father had been close as he was growing up, though as a successful physician, Wallace often worked long hours and missed some of the important events in the little boy's daily life. When he was five, Andy's stated ambition was to be a doctor, "like my dad," and later his inclination toward science, increasingly evident in his classes, supported the probability that entering medicine or an allied field would be the right choice.

In his early teen years, Andy, like most kids his age, became interested in the issue of procreation. As part of the ongoing family conversation about adoptive issues, Andy had been told that Emma and Wallace decided to adopt because they had been unable to conceive a biological child. They explained that they had never been able to determine just why they were an infertile couple. The many specialists they had consulted had been unable to pinpoint a specific cause—and thus unable to suggest a treatment. Emma and Wallace finally chose adoption as the way to have the family they wanted.

One afternoon after school, when Andy was helping his mother do the weekly grocery shopping, he asked her about something that had been on his mind for weeks. "How do I know I'll be fertile if it happened to you and Dad?" Emma was surprised by her son's question, which disrupted her concentration on selecting the perfect melon for dessert. She couldn't think how to answer Andy, but she knew that he had asked a fair question, and one that must be important to him. She said only, "Let's talk about it later, when we've finished with our shopping."

The family had a talk that evening after dinner. Andy listened to his parents' attempts to reassure him. Even if their own infertility did have a physical cause, Andy could not have inherited it; his genes were those of his (fertile) birth parents. Andy appeared to understand what they were saying, but he also seemed to want to stress the difference between his birth heritage of fertility and his adoptive heritage of infertility. "Thank God I wasn't born from you and Daddy," was his final hurtful comment.

Over the next months, Andy, always a tease albeit in a good-hearted way, began to torment his father with remarks that had a cruel edge. For example, he made disparaging jokes about the heavy horn-rimmed glasses Wallace always wore. And one day, when his father came to the breakfast table wiping a bit of shaving cream off his earlobe, Andy said, "I'm glad I'm not ugly like you." His parents' silence was the strongest expression of their shock, but Emma recovered and began to berate the boy, while Wallace grinned in blushing embarrassment. The next time Andy made a negative comment about his father's looks, Wallace was ready. He had thought about the earlier occasion and rehearsed an appropriate reply. "I am glad that you—and by the way, your mother and I, too—appreciate your good looks. But I do not like the way you are using them to put me down. And I don't think you will like it either, once you think about it.

Now, that is enough about the subject." Andy looked uncomfortable and said no more.

Changes in Andy's behavior were not limited to his sarcastic comments to his father. He stopped being willing to go to the grocery story with his mother, and even avoided carrying the groceries in from the car when she got home. He withdrew from the fishing trips on which he had formerly accompanied his father when Wallace was able to take a few days off and get away from it all. Andy was frequently unable to participate in family activities because he had "things" to do at school. No one in the family could ascertain what those things were, because he had become very protective of his privacy. His parents were not allowed into his room without his permission. He had transformed it into a gallery of rock stars, even putting posters up on the ceiling so he could look up at his new idols while he was lying in bed listening to their music at full blast. A concert two hundred miles away by the Grateful Dead was more important than the annual anniversary party given for his parents by their friends.

Andy's father was more hurt by the wall Andy seemed to be putting up than was his mother. Emma was not surprised that Andy's former love and admiration for his parents seemed temporarily to be disappearing. She had intuitively expected that he would want to withdraw from the openly expressed, affectionate family relationships that they had enjoyed when he was younger. She recognized that he was testing his growing desire for autonomy. "It's to be expected at his age," she reassured her husband. Perhaps because he had been able to spend less time with Andy in his younger years, Wallace minded the loss of his son's companionship more than did Emma. And of course, Andy's attitude was more painful for his father, for he was the primary target of the teenager's struggle to assert his independence.

Wallace and Emma talked over their concern about their son's hostility and decided the best course was to adopt an attitude of "wait and see." It would serve them well.

Andy's problem was a complex one. It began with his fear of being like his father, whom he had always admired, because of his father's infertility problem. Though that weighed on his mind, he was also aware, and glad, that he could expect to escape his father's fate. Thus his irrational fear was compounded by a hidden sense of guilt, hidden even from himself, over being a survivor, in the Darwinian sense of the word, and besting his father in this particular measure of manliness. Andy's double-edged conflict is common in the teenage children of infertile adoptive parents.

Beyond all that, Andy was also apprehensive that he might not do as well in his future career as his highly successful father. That competitive reaction is not uncommon in the children, whether biological or adoptive, of outstanding achievers. But Andy's solution to his many-layered conflict, his use of his adoptive status as a hostile weapon to effect his withdrawal from his father, created even further problems.

On another occasion, in a conversation with his parents, Andy chose to express his sarcastic thanks to the deity who kept him from being just like his father. At the dinner table, Emma innocently inquired why Andy had decided not to continue his concentration on science in his last year of high school. Andy turned away from his mother and looked directly at his father as he paused for maximum dramatic effect. "Thank God, *I* am going to be really rich! I will be a stockbroker like my other father." Andy knew that his adoption records noted his birth father's occupation as stockbroker. He continued in the same unkind vein. "If you were my genetic father, Daddy, I would have to be bald like you in a couple of years. I would wear horn-rimmed glasses. I would have to be a doctor. Oh, no, no. Not for me."

Wallace calmly ignored the barbs concealed in his son's outburst. He said reassuringly, "You don't have to choose the same career as mine. You know how your mother and I feel about choices." That was Wallace's way of reminding Andy that because he had been adopted by parents who believed that a child should be as free to choose as the parents are to afford, he already had the freedom in regard to his education and future career that he seemed to feel he had to seize from his parents. But, of course, it was important to Andy to feel that he had the ability to take it for himself.

What happened to Andy's sunny disposition when he became a teenager? His parents wistfully asked each other that question more than once. He had always been a tease, true enough, but why did his teasing suddenly take a mean turn? His mother conjectured that Andy might feel secretly humiliated about once having been given away. Many years earlier, he had confided to her his belief that he had been born to a married couple who gave him away because they thought there was something wrong with him. Paraphrasing a song that had been popular at the time of her own engagement, Emma said, "He just couldn't imagine a couple not being married. At that age, parents go together in marriage like a horse goes with a carriage."

Though it took time, Emma and Wallace were able to help Andy regain his equilibrium and complete his passage into adulthood. They relied on the simple but demanding (of them) method of not finding fault with him, not losing their tempers with him. They vowed not to retaliate punitively, but steadfastly to maintain their patience. They supported each other's resolve.

Andy's attitude of derogation and withdrawal nevertheless lasted into his college years. But Emma noticed, sometime during his sophomore year, that her son began to change in subtle ways. First, he began to show renewed appreciation for some of their actions; he thanked them for the humorous Valentine they sent that winter, and told them he felt lucky they had bought him a computer for his class work. Then, without telling them beforehand, he unexpectedly came home to attend their annual anniversary party. At spring break, he told his mother that he wanted to bring his roommate home and warned her he had already boasted about what a good cook she was. He stopped picking on his father and instead reminisced about the fun they had when they went fishing together when he was a kid.

Once Andy declared peace, his parents again began to enjoy his company. They no longer felt they had to be on guard, and began to relax in the improved family atmosphere. The climax of their happiness came at the beginning of their son's senior year of college, when Andy informed a stunned Wallace and Emma that he had decided that he did after all want to go into medicine. The only problem was, he would have to spend an additional year as an undergraduate to make up for the science courses he had missed. He hoped they wouldn't object to the additional expense. "I don't mind telling you," confessed Emma, "we were the happiest people in the world at that moment. Of course, we tried to act nonchalant, but we were certainly pleased by this very unexpected news." And part of his parents' happiness came from their realization that through communicating their faith in the basic goodness and strength of their family ties, and their patience while Andy tested them and himself as an adopted son, they had indeed been able to help.

9 Discipline

When adoptive mother Faith Nevins recognizes a situation in which her little girl obviously needs to be disciplined, she is often seized by an irrational fear. "Will my Carla love me less?" is her unreasoning anxiety about her parental responsibility to guide, protect, set a good example, and administer punishment. Although Faith says she would never really ask herself "something so ridiculous," the truth is that even so small an action as putting out a hand to restrain her three-year-old daughter from grabbing another child's toy can create in her a fleeting sense of uneasiness.

Sound silly? Not in the least! Because all children *are* less loving at the moment they are being disciplined. In the eyes of any child, adopted or not, the parent who hands out any kind of discipline, ranging from mild restraint to a spanking, has suddenly become the HATED one, the BAD parent of childish fantasy. Although adoption is irrelevant to this ordinary reaction, research shows that adoptive parents, as a group, are more concerned than others about how their children feel towards them when discipline is necessary.

One father put the dichotomy faced by adoptive parents this way: "You must completely forget about the adoption if you want to live your life with your children—and it must be on your mind all along." (L. Peller, 1962: 1–14). Adoptive parents do not take the emotional fulfillment of parenthood for granted. Natural as it is for them to want to forget the emptiness of the time before the child joined the family, they cannot overlook the fact that what is now theirs came from the relinquishment of another. Moreover, for the sake of their child's developing sense of self, remembering the birth mother's relinquishment is a sacred duty. But having to remember that fact all along makes it more difficult for adoptive parents to be natural and spontaneous when discipline is called for.

Styles of Discipline

For young ones, learning about physical and social limits and how to regulate behavior does not come naturally. Acquiring good eating habits and going to bed at the right time, tolerating the frustrations of the nursery world and getting along with others through give and take: these are behaviors that a child must learn, and the process of learning often goes against the child's inclinations. The chief source of such learning is usually the child's mother, and one of the primary teaching tools is discipline.

Parents usually have a characteristic approach to discipline that remains the same over the years; it seems that the choice of a way to train a child is as firm a personality trait as food preferences or speech patterns. That means, of course, that parents who want to change their disciplinary style will have to make a concerted effort to break old habits.

The discipline that parents, either biological or adoptive, mete out to their children can be divided into three broad categories. One style of discipline is the authoritarian approach. The authoritarian parent simply says to the child, "Do as you are told." Typically, little or no explanation for the edict is offered. The child learns from experience that punishment—often the corporal kind—will result if obedience is not forthcoming.

A second style of discipline is termed laissez-faire. "Do whatever you want to do," says the laissez-faire parent. This approach can be deceptive, because it seems to offer the child a choice. Yet it really offers little more than a vacuum of authority. The child is left to rely on his or her own immature judgment, which is very likely to be unequal to the task at hand.

A third style of discipline, and the one recommended by most professionals who work with children, is the child-centered approach. The parent who uses the child-centered style of discipline tries to accomplish two goals: to express to the child an understanding of the behavior that has necessitated the discipline; and to give reasons the child can understand for adopting the desired behavior. "It is better for you to do your homework now, even though you would rather go out to play, because then you will be prepared for your class tomorrow and you will feel good about going to school." That statement appeals to a child's pragmatic sense of reality. It is a reminder that consequences follow upon acts and omissions. Moreover, the parent's implicit sharing of authority—because a child knows full well that a parent is not obliged to offer a reason for issuing an order—is a powerful stimulus to the child's sense of self-esteem. So is the parental sharing in the child's wish to have pleasure now and put off work until later. The child-centered approach to discipline also strengthens the child's wish to identify with the parent, and the parent's understanding, goodness, and self-control.

The cartoon by Charles Saxon (*The New Yorker*, August 10, 1981) sets up an amusing model for discussing the three styles of discipline. It shows a child of five seated at the dinner table with her parents. She is stubbornly refusing to eat. The father says, "Let's review the whole picture, Janine. You don't like milk. You don't like chicken. You don't like anything green. Now, you tell me, Janine—what does that leave us with?" What do you think is likely to happen next at this family's dinner table? Will Janine be sent to her room without any supper—the authoritarian approach? Will she get to skip her well-balanced meal and eat pizza instead—the laissez-faire approach? Or will her father go on to use the child-centered approach? He might, for example, say to his daughter, "I know you don't like the chicken and vegetables, but you do like ice cream. So how about a compromise . . . after you eat the food that is good for you, you can eat the food you enjoy." Another child-centered choice would be to give Janine permission to leave the table if she doesn't want to eat, with the understanding that she can return to finish her meal (chicken and vegetables included) at any time that the rest of the family is still eating dinner.

Janine's father can take credit for following the first rule of constructive communication in the parent-child conflict situation: he does address the problem in a calm and low key manner. He also follows the second rule, which is to name the problem clearly. He helps Janine understand the way he is planning to attack the problem, through his concrete declaration, "Let's review." Where he has erred is in using a complaint to appeal to Janine's still largely undeveloped sense of reality. And this father omits the final, and most critical, step in the communication between parent and child in a conflict situation. He fails to give the child several constructive alternatives, from which she is allowed to choose just one solution to her problem.

When the Adoptive Parent Must Discipline

Research into the way adoptive parents discipline their children indicates that they often have problems coping with their child's frustration and anger, and may therefore be overly permissive. Does that mean that Janine will get pizza if she is an adopted daughter? The reader must decide that one!

When adoptive parents must administer discipline, the inevitable conflict between parent and child is further complicated by the adoptive situation. The feelings, attitudes and imaginings of the adopted child must be taken into account, as well as those of the adoptive parent.

Talking about the adoptedness issue at the time it intrudes into the conflict situation can help a child to distinguish between the two. For example, a child who does not want to wear a school uniform might claim that the birth mother would surely not insist on it. The adoptive parent should address the child's confusion of issues by first pointing out the necessity of respecting the school's authority and then adding that living with a birth mother does not exempt pupils from wearing the school uniform. This firm clarification of the two aspects of the child's remark will help the child differentiate between the conflict over the school uniform and the adoptedness issue. Ideally, the situation should be handled in a way that conveys the message that the parent loves the child but not the behavior that is causing the conflict.

A common disciplinary technique is the threat of banishment. Many children have been told by an impatient and annoyed parent, "I am going to send you back to the Indians." The boy who hears this from his biological mother as he is dawdling in front of the magazine rack in the supermarket correctly interprets her remark to mean, "Hurry up, I am getting tired of waiting for you." The adopted child, however, may well take the threat literally, due to the feelings evoked by the original act of parental abandonment. A child who was once given away can never take the threat of banishment lightly, and thus it should be avoided entirely by adoptive parents.

Another disciplinary technique that adoptive parents should try to avoid is the "silent treatment." As an adult, Mary Jane remembered that her adoptive mother usually did not talk to her for several hours after she had been naughty. This behavior made young Mary Jane extremely frightened and panicky. "Talk to me, talk to me," she would beg her mother. At such times, the little girl felt totally abandoned. That, of course, was not her mother's intention. She simply disciplined Mary Jane in the same manner as her own (biological) mother had disciplined her: the silence was meant to be a small punishment for minor infractions. She had not realized that to her adopted daughter, silence created a feeling of unbearable isolation associated with early, half-forgotten moments in a children's home before her adoption. For any child, parental silence is a form of abandonment. The difference between the adopted child and the child in the biological family lies in the intensity of the feelings of abandonment the silence creates.

Another common technique of parental discipline is belittling the naughty child. That technique, too, should be avoided by adoptive parents. The adoptee, who already feels less worthy because of the birth parents' original act of relinquishment, tends to confuse the adoptive parent's belittling behavior with the birth parent's past actions. For example, one twelve-year-old adoptee faced a conflict with his father because the boy was not spending enough time on his homework. The adoptive father, always explosive of temper and now feeling frustrated and inadequate because he was unable to change his son's attitude, angrily knocked the boy's stamp collection, the cherished object of the energies that should first have gone into his homework, onto the floor. It was natural for the boy to interpret the action as a gesture of powerful disrespect for himself—the same way he interpreted, in his innermost thoughts, the action of his birth parents in giving him away. The incident with his adoptive father did not help the boy learn to spend more time on his studies, but only to question his self-worth.

A disciplinary technique that works especially well with older children when conflict situations arise is offering a compromise solution that involves some freedom of choice and some acceptance of constraint. A good example can be seen in the case of Mitch Steele, adopted at the age of three months. When he was fourteen, Mitch informed his adoptive parents that henceforth they should call him Robert, the name his birth mother had selected for her baby. "He was adamant on the point," recalled Mitch's father, Bradley Steele. The Steeles were both surprised and upset by Mitch's choice, which seemed like a rejection of their authority—and their love.

Despite their distress, Bradley and Barbara were able to handle the confrontation with Mitch through a child-centered approach. They told their son that he was free to call himself whatever he chose outside the house, but that they would continue to call him by the name they had given him. He would simply have to accept that fact.

Mitch's campaign to change the name he was called by other people was not very successful. His friends respected his request but could not remember to call him Robert. Within weeks, Mitch gave up his attempt, but his parents perceived his disappointment. Meanwhile, they had been able to cope with their own hurt feelings by recognizing that their son's desire to take back his birth name was fundamentally the expression of his desire for some degree of autonomy; it had only incidentally challenged their authority and had not been intended as a rejection of their love for him. In the hope of demonstrating to Mitch that they too valued his birth heritage, the Steeles suggested that their son should take Robert as a middle name.

Now it was Mitch's turn to be surprised. He loved his parent's suggestion, and immediately began to use the initial R. on official documents, such as his application for a learner's permit from the Bureau of Motor

Vehicles. Interestingly, he also decided to keep the middle name his adoptive parents had given him, which was Kevin. When he applied for a Social Security card that summer, he gave his full name as Mitchell Kevin Robert Steele.

Wanting to use the name given by a birth parent often is the way that an adoptee expresses the burgeoning adolescent need for self-assertion, selecting a gesture that is unavailable to a teenager growing up with biological parents. Unfortunately, the adoptee's tactic hits the adoptive parents where they are most vulnerable, in their sense of entitlement to be parents. The child seems to be saying, "I am not yours!"

A second significance of the desire to use a name selected by the birth parents is that it represents the youngster's way of coming to terms with the emotional vulnerability of the adoptive situation and thoughts such as "I was given away once." The name given by birth parents can bring the comforting feeling that "They did love me ... some ... at least enough to give me a name."

How Adopted Children Perceive Parents in Time of Conflict

Most of us no longer remember that once we saw each of our own parents as two very different people. Yet researchers in the field of child development believe that is just how the child reacts emotionally. Two images of the parent exist. One is the "good" parent, the loving indulgent one; the other is the "bad" parent, who thwarts the child and acts angry. When the good parent is present, the bad parent has vanished; when the bad parent appears, the good parent is nowhere in sight.

Investigators of the psychology of the adoptee believe that adopted children may be especially challenged by the natural tendency of all children to see each parent as two different people. When a child is frustrated by an adoptive parent's disciplinary action, it is all too easy to imagine a loving birth parent who would do everything the child wants. In the adopted child's mind, the good parent is not an alternate version of the adoptive parent who is administering discipline, but rather the imagined birth parent.

The child in the biological family eventually must come to terms with the fact that one parent can be both *good* and *bad*; eventually, the images of the two parents can be integrated into one perception of Mother or Dad. For the adoptee, that realistic integration can be difficult to achieve. In times of conflict at home, the adoptive parent is the bad parent; at other times, it is the birth mother who abandoned the child who becomes the bad parent. The child is thus able to cling to false expectations—which lead to repeated disappointments.

Testing the Adoptive Parents

The experience of Mitch's parents, Bradley and Barbara Steele, is an example of the vulnerability of adoptive parents—one of the reasons they often have difficulty in administering appropriate discipline. Although Mitch's announced intention of using the name given him by his birth mother was meant primarily as an act of self-assertion, it probably also contained an element of parental testing.

Some children test and re-test their adoptive parents. They engage in behavior that appears—often *is—*

openly provocative of the parent's anger. The real purpose of such behavior is to gain the reassurance that the parent truly loves the adoptee. A backward way of going about things, perhaps, but one that appeals to many a child. The provocative behavior acts as camouflage for the child's real concern, which is that the parent toward whom the behavior is directed is indifferent.

Although children who thus test their parents usually do not understand the motive for their own actions, they do feel reassured when they see the parent react, either positively or negatively, to the testing behavior. A firm response, even if it's an angry one, is proof positive, in the child's view of logic, that the parent really does care. Permissiveness is usually interpreted by the child as indifference. Sadly, the adoptive parent often operates under a different set of logical assumptions. Fearing that an angry response will be perceived by the child as a lack of love, the parent struggles to remain impassive, thus leaving the child without the reassurance he or she was seeking.

Testing behavior is frequently evoked by an act of discipline. When an adopted youngster responds to discipline by declaring angrily, "You're not my real parents!", it is often a testing maneuver. The child is really saying, "You are bad because you won't let me do what I want to do." The parent should respond to the specific disciplinary issue in the usual way; at the same time, the parent must also affirm, "Yes, I am your real parent." At that emotional moment, it may be wiser to say no more about the issue. Later, at a calmer time, the family should consider together what it means to be a *real* parent. It may be appropriate to continue the discussion by looking at the concept of the real child in the real family.

The behavior of testing is more likely to occur with the adoptee who comes to the family as an older child, and has therefore missed those earlier nurturing experiences that secure most firmly the relationship between parent and child. Nevertheless, testing behavior may also occur in adoptees who have lived their entire lives with their adopted families—indeed, it may occur in children in biological families as well. It may even be a good sign when a child "tests." It means that the youngster is actively working to try to strengthen family ties, even if the method chosen is slightly misguided, and definitely wearing on the parents.

Youngsters who were adopted when they were older have already been through repeated experiences of rejection and frustration. Such adoptees may dump on their adoptive parents the feelings of hatred they have for the birth parents, whom they hold responsible for the unhappiness of their young lives. An example can be seen in Paul Jones, a boy whose early years were spent in a series of foster homes and one orphanage. He was adopted at the age of nine by a family with two grownup biological sons, and he is now twelve years old. One day, while his mother was in the kitchen fixing lunch, Paul took apart the jigsaw puzzle she had been working on all morning, and started to put it back together himself. His father Arthur, home to share lunch with his family, scolded Paul for his action. "That was a thoughtless thing to do," he said angrily.

Later that day, Paul retaliated against his father's act of discipline by telling neighbors across the street that the Joneses are not his "real" parents. As a dramatic afterthought, he added that Arthur Jones had beaten him just that morning. The neighbors, who had known the Jones family for many years, were absolutely certain that Arthur Jones would not beat his son. They telephoned Arthur that evening to let him know about Paul's reckless accusation.

Arthur Jones handled the ensuing confrontation with his son very carefully. He began by reviewing the events of the day, starting with Paul's behavior at lunch and the reprimand he received. He went on to give Paul the details of the neighbor's telephone call. "It is always okay to tell the truth," he reassured Paul, "and there's nothing wrong with telling people you are adopted if you want to." But, he added, he thinks that Paul must have been very angry about being scolded at lunchtime, and so he used the truth like a weapon to get back at his father. Paul had implied that because he was adopted, he was not a real son of the family. That, Arthur Jones stated firmly, is not true.

Paul kept his face averted and did not respond to his father's lecture, but Arthur felt certain his words were well-understood nevertheless. So he went on to address the second issue involved. "Your story about the beating was an out-and-out lie. You are not to lie again, or punishment will follow. Lying is spreading trouble," concluded Arthur Jones. "I'll not have you do that."

Talking it over later with a counselor, Arthur and his wife Debbie agree that it may be true that Paul doesn't yet believe they are his "real" parents. "He had so many bad experiences before he came to us," reflected Debbie. "We had to make up to him for everything that he had suffered . . . even things we didn't know about." She paused, then continued, "We always have tried though, because we know it is harder on him than it is on us. He is the vulnerable, hurt child, after all—and sometimes, that is the only thought that keeps us going." She sums things up. "Things *are* better now. He doesn't lie any more, or twist things the way he used to. We have hopes that eventually he'll feel that he really does belong to us."

Separating the Issue of Adoption from the Disciplinary Conflict

It can sometimes be extremely difficult for a parent to separate the issues pertaining to adoption from those pertaining to the problem requiring discipline. An example can be seen in the behavior of Harriet, aged fourteen, who used words as weapons in a fight with her brother Travis, three years younger. Born to different birth parents, both children had been adopted in infancy by Jack and Billie Ballerdo. The children's fight began for reasons that had nothing to do with the adoption issue, and yet the fact that they were adopted colored the fight and called for careful handling by their mother.

Billie, weeding her garden, was assailed by the sound of loud voices one afternoon. She hurried into the kitchen to find brother and sister arguing in front of the refrigerator. Harriet was furious with Travis. She was looking at the battered remains of the chocolate cake meant for the party she was giving that evening in honor of her best friend, Nancy, who was moving with her family at the end of the month to another state. Harriet had just caught her brother in the act of demolishing her cake, and he seemed to be taking her own distress very casually. The least he could do, Harriet thought, was try

to rectify his misdeed by offering to go to the bakery to
get another cake before the party started. Travis remained seemingly indifferent to his sister's anger. Finally, Harriet shouted at him in a rage, "You . . . you
bastard!"

Billie told the children to stop shouting and asked
them for an explanation. Harriet denounced her brother's act in ruining the party cake, and Billie responded
by telling Travis he should be ashamed of himself. She
added that he must go pick up another cake before the
party started and told Travis that his allowance would
be docked as a punishment for his thoughtless action.
Then she turned to her daughter. "Why did you use that
word, Harriet? 'Bastard' . . . where did you learn that?"

Mollified by her mother's quick action to save her
party and her obvious concern that justice be meted out,
the now quieter Harriet defended herself, "Everybody
says it. I hear it on TV, too."

"What does it really mean?" asked Travis.

Billie Ballerdo explained, "In the old days, many
people believed that children should not be born until
after the parents were legally married. The word was
used to mean children of parents who weren't married
to one another . . . like Jason," she noted, referring to the
infant son of an unmarried couple in the neighborhood.
Billie continued, "Ideas have changed, but the word was
used as an insult in the old days, and I don't want you
two to insult each other." She faced Travis directly.
"Travis, you insulted your sister by your greedy behavior, and by acting like what she wanted to do for her
friend was of no importance. And Harriet," Billie added,
turning to her daughter, "you insulted Travis by calling

him a bastard. Don't insult each other in the future . . . I mean that!"

Billie later confessed that she had been so angry with both her son and her daughter at the time that she was afraid she might not have dealt with the situation in the best and most constructive way. The disciplinary problem was not quickly solved, for the two children continued to fight until they were almost out of adolescence, with Travis often acting like a "brat" and Harriet frequently taking herself too seriously. But Billie was right to confront the issue of illegitimacy raised by Harriet's remark, and her prompt response was reassuring to both children, even though it contained a note of anger. Children raised in a biological family might use the word bastard to mean simply that a brother or sister is acting disagreeable. But for adoptees, there is always an additional meaning that evokes feelings of unworthiness associated with the birth circumstances. If Billie Ballerdo had allowed her daughter's remark to go unchallenged, she would have given tacit agreement to Harriet's attempt to hurt Travis by referring to the unhappy background of his adoption. And, of course, that would have permitted Harriet to hurt herself as well, since she, too, was born out of wedlock.

Billie was also right to try to deal with the situation in a rational manner, even though she was upset herself. Although her behavior may have been somewhat emotional, she nevertheless gave her children an example of reasoned thinking, and a demonstration of how reason, in itself, can both clarify and comfort. The adoptive mother had conveyed to her children her own good intentions, her wish to make a difficult situation better for them, and her goal of helping both of them master their destructive and self-destructive impulses. Children will absorb such a parental attitude, and retain it, until eventually it crystallizes inside them as an identification with the good qualities of the parent. It becomes part of the child's inner strength throughout life.

Crucial to Billie's successful handling of the situation was her own ability to separate the two issues that confronted her simultaneously: the ordinary conflict that called for the administration of discipline, and the adoptive issue that called for reasoned language and emotional support. She dealt with the squabble between the two children in the usual way, by trying to mete out justice. She administered a common form of punishment in the family by withholding Travis's allowance, and telling Harriet to apologize for insulting her brother—as she would have done if Harriet had called him a "jerk" or a "creep" or some other insult that didn't involve the issue of adoption. At the same time, Billie displayed a sensitivity to the fact that for adopted children, the word bastard is more than an ordinary insult. She gave them information about the historical context of the word and how it originally came to be viewed as an insult. Billie also told them how the social context has changed, so that being a bastard is no longer the shame and scandal it once was. At a deeper level of meaning, she rebuked her daughter for her aggressive use of the term and confronted the girl's derogation of her brother—and her own self-derogation—for being born to unmarried parents.

It is not unusual for older adoptees to use their adoptive status as weapons in fights with siblings, and parents must judge carefully whether or not such jousting calls for parental intervention. Fifteen-year-old Mary and her brother Lewis, sixteen, were bickering over their evening chores when Lewis proclaimed, "My natural mother and father were both lawyers!" Mary took on the challenge and responded, "Mine were college graduates." Lewis further boasted, "Our parents wanted me because they adopted me first. They just got you because of me." Mary, an inch taller than her older brother, had the last word. "You are growing up to be just a shrimp. So there!"

The parents of this brother and sister wisely stayed out of the fight. Although the adoptive situation was the basis of the children's remarks, it was obvious that neither one was hurt by the other's comments and that both were able to accept being adopted as one reality of their lives, like height or hair color or scholastic achievements, or any of the other differences between people.

The Vulnerability of Adoptive Parents

Just as adoption is a lifelong issue for adopted children, so it will always be an issue for adoptive parents. And nothing is more likely to highlight this vulnerability of the parents than the situation of disciplining the child. "I hate to admit just how insecure I can sometimes be," says Lola Stark.

The Starks were a family of three: Joe, Lola, and their adopted daughter Willa. Joe and Lola had adopted Willa at birth, bringing her home the day she was released from the hospital. They felt they were unusually fortunate because Willa's temperament very much resembled Lola's, and the girl even looked like one of her cousins, the child of Joe's younger sister. The Starks were a close-knit and loving family.

As Willa entered adolescence, there was one major problem between her and her mother, which was Willa's sloppiness around the house. Lola felt increasingly frustrated by her inability to make her thirteen-year-old daughter understand that her behavior was not just bothersome but also inconsiderate. One day, Lola was in the kitchen preparing an elaborate meal for dinner guests, when Willa came home from school. Lola watched her daughter drop two apple cores in the big crystal ashtray on the living room coffee table; out in the hallway, she could see Willa's snow-covered boots leaving puddles on the freshly polished wood floor.

Lola was furious at this latest example of her daughter's thoughtlessness and lack of respect for Lola's standards and wishes. Yet even as her anger built, she was aware of a hesitation about confronting Willa over the issue. Lola knew it was irrational, but somehow she thought of the girl's unknown birth mother, and feared that Willa might decide she wanted to go live with her instead of the Starks. Of course, Willa had never even mentioned any interest in her birth mother, yet somehow Lola couldn't get the notion out of her head.

She wanted to initiate a calm discussion of Willa's inconsiderate behavior, but her feelings were heating up to the point that she felt like crying rather than talking about the matter rationally. And Willa, whose closeness to her mother made her able to sense her feelings even before they were expressed, had already retreated into a stubborn silence.

Looking at the sulky girl, Lola felt certain Willa knew what she had done, and why her mother was angry. It was just too much! Impulsively, Lola discharged the tension she was feeling.

"You don't love us because we are not your natural parents!"

She could have bitten out her tongue, but the words were already spoken.

Lola later realized she had taken the offensive as a way of defending herself against the accusations she feared Willa would make—that she was a "witch" to insist on absolute neatness in the living room. What should have been a simple issue of discipline regarding her daughter's bad habit of sloppiness had turned into a hurtful conflict involving the adoptive situation. Lola's own deeply hidden questions about her entitlement to be a parent had colored her behavior. She knew that she should have dealt with the issue of the mess Willa had made with her boots and her apple cores, not only by explaining again why it was thoughtless and disrespectful, but perhaps also by administering some punishment, such as requiring the girl to clean up the mess, or putting the living room off limits for a time, or docking her allowance for each episode of sloppiness in the shared living space. Instead, she had wounded her daughter, and inflamed her own doubts about her entitlement as a parent.

In the context of the Starks' loving and supportive family relationship, the difficulty caused by Lola's hidden doubts was relatively slight. Willa continued in her sloppy ways until she married, when she became more like her mother in her habits. That type of change— eventually becoming like a parent one has previously defied—is characteristic of many young people, whether growing up as adopted or biological family members. In Willa's case, the change represented a final putting away of childish behavior, the achievement of autonomy, a signal that she was irrevocably joining the world of adults.

Years later, Willa revealed that she never forgot her mother's unfortunate remark. It had filled her with a sense of guilt that took a long time to dissipate. The guilt was not, of course, about her sloppy habits, but rather the implication that she was not grateful for the gifts of love and nurturance the Starks had lavished on her. It took Willa a long time to understand and sympathize with the doubts and fears that had prompted her mother to utter those words.

10 Sex and Commitment

Learning about sex means more than merely acquiring factual information about reproductive physiology. Closely linked to sex are a number of social and psychological issues of great importance to the growing child. Sex education means grasping the nature of the blood tie between parent and child. It means understanding the nature of sexuality and sexual relationships, such as those between one's parents. It also means learning about gender, the social definitions of being male or female. Finally, it means learning the social standards that are applied to matters of gender, sexuality, and reproduction.

In our culture, sex is considered to be a private matter. Therefore information on the subject may be restricted, especially for children. Some schools do teach sex education, but in deference to parental concerns about their children's readiness, the course tends to be taught in junior high or high school, when most students have already acquired a good deal of information—or misinformation—through more informal means. Children are likely to turn to their parents to help clear up their concerns about the sexual matters they have observed, guessed at, or learned from their peers. And their parents are likely to be the best teachers in regard to the complex social and psychological aspects of sexual matters.

Parents of adopted children have no choice but to teach them early in life about sexual issues. They cannot leave the task to the educational system, because no school class gives informative yet comforting answers to questions that deeply affect the life of the adoptee. The child's first concern is usually about his or her own self: "Why was I adopted?" is asking, what does it mean about me? Later, the interest broadens, and "Why was I adopted?" means, what were the circumstances, in the lives of my birth parents and my adoptive parents, that made it necessary for me to be adopted?

The Issue of Commitment

The United States, as a cultural melting pot, embraces a wide variety of social standards in regard to appropriate sexual behavior. One point about which everyone agrees, however, is that procreation should be linked to a commitment to the welfare and happiness of the child that will be born. The social ideal for procreation is the married couple with their joint emotional and financial resources, but in this day and age, we are willing to accept many variations—the unmarried couple, such as celebrities Farrah Fawcett and Ryan O'Neal; the single mother determined to raise her own child; even gay or lesbian couples who make a home for one partner's biological child—so long as the basic commitment is evident.

Consideration for others is an important component of the committed relationship, including the "other" who is as yet an unborn child. A growing boy or girl needs to learn about this at home, so as to develop the necessary motivation to control sexual desires later and to choose to delay sexual intimacy until emotional maturity is reached.

It is a generalization but nevertheless an accurate one to say that adoptive parents place an extremely high value on this kind of commitment to the family. Compared to the rest of society, they are likely to be more strongly committed to family relationships, and to be disapproving of the lack of commitment. The reasons for their attitudes are obvious. Most people adopt because they are unable to procreate; after years of trying to have a child, it is hard for them to sympathize with those who take the act of conception so lightly they do it without commitment to the child who is the outcome of their action.

Moreover, as they go through the adoption process, they confront the many painful aspects of procreation without commitment. There is an indefinable but clearly evidenced sadness that pervades the pre-adoptive period. Thoughts of the unknown adoptee born into the situation are at the center of this sadness. In addition, prospective adoptive parents imagine the thoughts and feelings of the others involved in the adoptive situation. Whether or not they ever meet the birth mother face to face, they tenderly project the sense of loss that comes from conceiving and giving birth to a child who cannot be kept, and the agony of having to make such a decision. They think about the birth father, including the one who must forever be unknowable because the birth mother can't or won't divulge his identity. Putting themselves in his place, they wonder how he might feel if he knew what was happening, how he might cry, "If only I had been told! I would have tried to do the right thing!" They reflect on the plight of the birth grandparents, whose hearts must be forever empty of the joys of that particular wonderful child. They think about the hardship of the foster mother's role, in giving the best possible care to the children who will be in her charge only temporarily. They recognize that even the professionals involved in the adoption may worry about making the correct decisions to insure the future welfare of the helpless child. No, adoptive parents can never avoid the recognition of the human pain that is inevitably the foundation for the joyous ceremony in which a child is "reborn" to a new mother and father.

Although they try to hide it from themselves and their friends, John and Zena Lopez cannot avoid the pain that is mingled with their joy. Watch Zena turn to her husband, saying, "Look, our child is so happy!"; watch him smile back at her to reassure her that her words are true. Yet still the pain crowds in. One of the friends with whom they are dining says, "That little one is so lucky . . . that you took him in, I mean." John and Zena exchange glances, embarrassed by the patronizing remark about their son, yet they smile politely. John replies firmly, "We are lucky to have him," while Zena wonders what it will be like for their three-year-old son when he is mature enough to ponder his beginnings in life. Will he be able to feel good about himself? About them? Will they be able to help him with his questions about his birth parents? Will he be able to understand the reasons he was adopted? To accept them?

The difficult task Zena and John face in raising their son is teaching him the importance of commitment to family responsibility while still honoring those who did not make such a commitment, his birth parents. What that requires from them is their own genuine understanding of the behavior of their son's birth parents, and the ability to accept and forgive its impact on their beloved boy. For children are quick to sense underlying disapproval and to see through attempts to cover it over. Strategies such as an evasion of the topic, or weak excuses for the behavior of the birth parents, will not work to give the adoptee the comfort his or her situation requires along with the social standards that will help the child as an adult avoid the same kind of pain. All children will feel themselves criticized when they hear others criticizing their parents—even their unknown birth parents. And because of their sensitivity, they tend to misinterpret even the innocuous words of others as criticism. Adoptive parents puzzle over how, without appearing either judgmental about the birth parents or hypocritical about their own standards, they can convey their message of the importance of linking sexual relationships with family commitment.

One other concern lies in the fact that too much attention to this theme of the link between sex and commitment could cause later problems, such as sexual inhibitions and a diminution of erotic pleasure when an adult. Overemphasis might also have the unfortunate effect of confirming the child in a negatively stereotyped self-image. "I must have 'bad blood'," the child may conclude. As a teenager, this may evolve into a fear that the birth parents were "oversexed" and that such a tendency could be inherited. Of course, neither belief is accurate. As research studies confirm, there is no reason to conclude that birth mothers who give their babies up for adoption are any more promiscuous, or sexually active, than other women their age. And excessive sexual appetite is not the result of genetic background but of faulty emotional development.

In most adoptive families, the dilemma of how to convey a gentle non-judgmental message about the sexual behavior of the birth parents surfaces sometime between the sixth and eighth year of the child's life. It is important to remember that the adoptee must be given information about such aspects of the birth background as the age, marital status, and family commitment of the birth parents as accurately as it is known, regardless of how the adoptive parents feel about these facts. Otherwise, the truth is almost sure to come out in some less desirable way. It will be found out from an old document tucked away in a drawer and long forgotten, or it may be casually mentioned by a relative who takes for granted that the child knows all the facts. A child who learns the facts about the status and motivations of birth parents in any other way than directly from the adoptive parents usually feels shocked and betrayed. For the loss of trust in the adoptive parents is far more destructive than anything the child might learn about the birth parents. In addition, the child may be burdened by a sense of personal devastation and shame. The accidental discoveries may make the child feel, "I must be bad if my (adoptive) parents believe that the behavior of my other parents was so bad they could not even tell me. . . ."

The Child's Own Judgments

Parents of school-age youngsters are confronted by a judgmental attitude that is more powerful at this age than at any other time of life. In all matters, the child will agree to no negotiation, recognizes no in-between. If things are not good, they must be bad. The intensity of the child's judgment at this age and the type of issue on which it can be brought to bear can be startling to adults, who have learned the art of compromise. An art teacher praised an eight-year-old girl who had drawn a figure with the arms larger than the torso. The teacher found the drawing intriguing and provocative. But the child, with her inflexible standards, had already characterized her picture as bad, because it lacked conventionality. She knew that she had not intended to make the arms so large, she simply lacked the skill to draw them to scale. The girl became visibly upset at the teacher's praise and wanted her to agree that the drawing was a poor one. Clearly, the child was not yet ready to tolerate a concept of deviation from the norm without attaching a judgment to it.

The adopted youngster of school age might focus the need to conform on the question, "Am I legal?" The child asking this question is seeking reassurance and wants it to be established beyond doubt that "I am the same as my friends." A simple answer—"Yes, you are legal, because we have legally adopted you, you are part of our family"—would suffice, especially when dealing with a child younger than about eight. An older adoptee might require a fuller answer, with specifics about the legal process of adoption. In either case, parents can remind the child of the explanations given at the first telling. Meanwhile, they can continue to affirm that, "Yes, indeed, you are most definitely legal. You are the same as your friends."

Older children often find a dictionary type of description of legal concepts not only reassuring but also intellectually stimulating. At about the age of ten, a child is ready to take an interest in abstract notions such as rights, privileges, and responsibilities. Even before that time, however, a youngster might find the concrete steps leading up to and culminating in the formal adoption ceremony intriguing. For example, the child who has been present at the adoption of a younger sibling gains a sense of emotional support through the experience. It gives ample proof of his or her own legality. Reading a book about the process can be helpful too. Fortunately, one is available in *Is That Your Sister?* (C. and S. Bunin, 1976). Written for the reader of six to eight years, but worthy also of an older child's interest, it is a copiously illustrated story about a trans-racial family going to court to complete a child's adoption.

Heredity and Environment

In the early years of our century, it was believed that environmental factors were the primary influence on the way a child turns out. A widely cited study of children who had been abandoned, comparing large samples of those who were soon adopted with those who remained institutionalized, was surprising in the clarity of its evidence that the IQ of the adopted children rose significantly over time in comparison to the IQ of the children who remained without families (Skeels, 1940: 281–308). Many other studies undertaken both in the United States and in other countries have since confirmed the powerful effect of the environment. One, carried out by Barbara Tizard in England, indicated that children adopted by

middle-class families attained a more successful adjustment than those who remained institutionalized or were
returned to their mothers, who were all from a lower
socioeconomic group (Tizard and Rees, 1974: 92–99).

Today, mounting evidence from genetic studies suggests that the growing child is also influenced by genetic
heritage. To what degree specific behavior is attributable
to either the factor of heredity or the factor of environment remains for the most part a mystery. Many adult
adoptees comment that they have always suspected the
importance of genetics. When they are successful in a
search for their blood relatives, adoptees report that they
find similarities in such things as careers, choice of
spouses, and hobbies that seem too close to be accidental. Among personal accounts, the book published by
English writer David Leitch is especially compelling
reading for adoptive families (Leitch, 1984).

The intuition that genetic inheritance is important
may be very upsetting to adoptees around the age of ten.
That harshly moral child tends to see things through a
dark glass anyway—unlike the adolescent, who, living
through a time of life when all is expectation and un-
tapped potential, may well hope for positive gifts from
the inherited genes. In the eyes of a younger child, the
birth mother's behavior that in actuality probably reflected the influence of a destructive environment on her
development is confused with a genetic imperative.

All school-age children, with their high moral standards and unwillingness to compromise are hurt when
the inevitable happens and they don't live up to their
own expectations. For adoptees, it doesn't matter that
the adoptive parents have communicated their own acceptance of the birth parent's behavior even though it

falls short of their own standards. The youngster believes, "My adoptive parents cannot possibly accept me, or my background, wholeheartedly, because of the way I came into the world." Children often keep their shame and dejection secret. They deny their feelings, hoping that they will go away. None of this means that the child in actuality is not well loved, nor that the child is unaware of the adoptive family's love and acceptance. But, at a certain moment, it does not seem to matter much.

Nine-year-old Yvette is an example of a child at risk for confusing her birth mother's behavior with her own self. When she was not quite six, her parents had gently and sensitively explained to her the meaning of various terms associated with adoption, and with illegitimacy as well. They had arranged for her to be invited to accompany another adoptive family to court to witness the ceremony of signing the adoption papers for a second child to join the family. Thanks to her parents' clear communication at the time of the original telling, Yvette already clearly understood the difference between her illegitimate birth and the legality of her adoptive status. But, like many adoptees, Yvette would need ongoing communication, with its combination of information and support, to help her through other periods of adjustment.

As Yvette's critical, evaluative, and judgmental capacities began to blossom, her formerly good opinion of herself started to diminish. She had begun to perceive that her self was rooted in the unsavory history of her birth mother's life. Even though her parents still shielded her from the most hurtful details, she knew enough to judge harshly.

Yvette had been an abandoned child. She had been born to a single sixteen-year-old drug abuser. When Yvette was twenty months old, her mother had left her alone in a dark hot room for several days, while a sweltering heat wave baked their city. "She might have died," said the physician to the policewoman who carried the inert infant to the hospital emergency room. Yvette had been found by neighbors, suffering from malnutrition and dehydration and covered with ugly sores; they called the police. During the week that Yvette had to remain in the hospital, the local news media picked up her story. Her birth mother was described as an "erratic" girl without any family support, who received welfare assistance. Although she had been offered mental health treatment more than once, she had always refused. She was charged with neglect of the child, and the presiding judge was quoted as saying, "Your behavior represents what is wrong with our times. You are irresponsible." He ordered Yvette to be placed under the care of a local social agency. Her birth mother seemed glad to give the child up, saying she did not want her any longer.

Once discharged from the pediatric ward, Yvette spent a few months with a foster family, where the redheaded toddler began to thrive. She was adopted soon afterward by Diane and Mel, and went to live with them in a town in the hill country of Texas. Eventually, she developed into a sturdy child who typically displayed an outgoing nature. At nine, she was still unaware of the heinous neglect she had suffered as a baby. "Perhaps we'll talk about it when she is completely grown up," said Diane, but at the moment she felt dubious that bringing up the truth could do her daughter any good. She noted that Yvette had apparently forgotten the events of her early life. The little girl seemed to have only one memory, more like a vague thought, of her birth mother. She told Diane, "I remember now . . . she was asleep on the bed. I was playing on the floor. She had red hair, or at least I think she did. I don't remember her face. That's all. . . ."

Though Yvette was probably unaware of any such feeling, the unseen face in her memory may well have inspired fear deep inside her. Behind its blankness (blank because she could not "see" it) no doubt would be depicted the history of her birth mother's life-threatening neglect of her. Yvette was beginning to ponder that indefinable part of herself that she intuitively knew was linked to her birth mother. It was more than just the red hair, although she could not say what it was.

Yvette, with her schoolgirl conscience at its high watermark, doubtless also felt pained that her birth mother failed to meet the high standards of her adoptive parents. Yvette had not yet reached the stage in her way of looking at things to imagine her parents could be more understanding than she, that they could comprehend the personal devastation associated with her birth mother's life. The notion that they could be more sympathetic than she to her birth mother's plight, if not to her behavior, had simply not occured to her.

Yvette would need additional guidance from her adoptive parents to learn how to make a distinction between herself, with her middle-class ultra-conventional (because of her age) goals, standards, and tastes, and her birth mother's "erratic" behavior. She had had no control over her birth mother's acts, yet she would be forever linked to them. Only through understanding that she was linked, and yet also could be separate, would

Yvette be able to achieve a sense of peaceful acceptance that could last her for the rest of her life.

Moments that imply a child's inarticulate plea for guidance can occur at any time, hidden in expressions of feeling that vary from the casual to the explosive. Yvette's plea was somewhere in the middle of the spectrum. It happened one afternoon, as she and her mother were walking along a cracked sidewalk to the office of Yvette's dentist, for her semi-annual checkup. They had stopped for a moment, so that Yvette could jump up and walk along the top of a stone wall in front of a well-kept house. Out the blue, as she teetered along the narrow wall, arms extended for balance, Yvette said, "I don't like my other mother." Momentarily nonplussed, Diane swallowed hard. Taking her daughter's hand and looking at her directly, face to face, she said, "Perhaps giving you up was the only thing she could do at the time." From atop the wall, Yvette stared at her mother as she interrupted her angrily. "Why wasn't she married, anyway? She could have got married!"

Diane took a few moments to think out her answer. It was hesitant, but as logical and positive as she knew how to make it. She hypothesized, "Yes, I suppose she could have. She probably loved your father, or at least I'm sure she thought she did . . . at first, anyway. The illegitimate part really had nothing to do with you." Yvette's expression became mournful as her mother's conversation touched more and more directly on her own negative feelings. "She was not thinking ahead at the time she got pregnant. She wasn't thinking about her future, and she wasn't thinking about yours, either. Maybe she couldn't talk to her mom about it. But she only wanted to have her baby. Afterwards, being a mother, that was something else. It's a job to be a parent, and she wasn't ready for it then."

Diane paused. She had not referred to the problems of neglect or drug abuse. She and Mel would wait until Yvette was many years older before revealing that information. To tell Yvette now would be to overload the girl with feelings of fear and anger. But Diane felt the need to say one more thing, to complete the conversation. "I don't think it was right for her to have a baby when she did. She should have waited. It would have been better for her, and better for her baby." Yvette looked at her mother. "I won't get pregnant until I'm all grown up and married," the girl said firmly.

"I know you won't, darling," answered Diane. Grasping Yvette's hand tightly, she helped her jump off the wall and watched as she hopped along the sidewalk on one foot. For the moment, Yvette had the information and the comfort she needed.

Children take their cues from their parents. In a family that encourages openness, the child feels, "My parents are there for me," and is more inclined to speak out about worries and problems. After her talk with Diane, Yvette felt relieved and more secure. She had learned that there were most likely extenuating circumstances to explain her birth mother's behavior, and she had received the reassurance that her mother did not judge her birth mother harshly. From Diane's demonstration of respect for the initial intentions of her birth mother, Yvette took an important lesson: a person's behavior is composed of a sequence of individual acts. Diane helped her daughter see that there were many different aspects of her birth mother's behavior: the feelings that led to the conception of a child, the decision to have the baby, and the later realization that she was not ready to be a mother. This helped Yvette make sense of the ambiguous circumstances of her early life, and helped her see that her birth mother's behavior was not entirely "bad." Looking for a brighter path is not an unreasonable approach when one is traveling through obscure territory.

Another significant aspect of Diane's communication was the way she concluded with a reference to her own standards, the ones she implicitly asked her daughter to accept. Moreover, she set up a situation that elicited from the girl an avowal of her own commitment to sexual responsibility. Bearing witness to one's future intentions is a good exercise that strengthens both present and future resolve. To speak a commitment is to strengthen and protect it; such is the power of speech.

Dealing with a Child's Confusions

The adopted youngster is interested in the sexual and procreative behavior of the adoptive parents as well as the birth parents. The child worries about the infertility of the adoptive parents, for example, especially if the issue has not been forthrightly and responsively explained. But it is often not easy to recognize when a child needs help in dealing with the information he or she receives. If children are confused, they may not directly express what is on their minds but may retreat fearfully into a silence that permits the confusion to grow.

Before reaching adolescence, many youngsters feel that the adult body is unattractive, because of their fear of the sexuality implicit in its contours. But children also fear any kind of imperfection or difference, especially if it can be viewed as "ugly." For example, children often draw back in horror upon first seeing a scar, such as that left by surgery or a burn. An adult may view a scar as the badge of a life-saving operation and display it proudly, but children view it primarily as a mutilation.

How a scar on her mother's stomach confused one adoptee is illustrated in the story that Hilda, an adoptee now in her forties, told about herself as a growing girl. Hilda's mother had a convoluted and badly discolored scar that was the result of an emergency appendectomy that saved her life when she was a teenager. Hilda had seen this hideous scar from her earliest childhood, when she sat on the bed and watched her mother getting dressed. But the girl failed to notice a second scar on her mother's body, left when she underwent surgery again after suffering recurring fibroid tumors of the uterus; her doctor recommended a complete hysterectomy. (This drastic treatment is in most cases frowned on today, but it was common in her mother's youth.)

It is not surprising that Hilda interpreted the disfiguring appendectomy scar as the reason for her adoptive mother's inability to bear children. But she was silent about her confusion, and her mother did not explain the real facts to Hilda. She remained silent partly because she was unaware of her daughter's mistaken idea, and partly because she had not yet come to terms with her own feelings about the hysterectomy that was the true cause of her infertility. She had learned that the medical profession was beginning to disavow the very treatment that had deprived her of her reproductive capability, and she reacted by denying rather than mourning her loss.

Hilda subsequently embroidered her confusion. She somehow arrived at the conclusion that the scar, which she viewed as a hideous mutilation, must have happened when her mother was attacked by a man, perhaps even her father. It was not until she was fully grown and actively sought help through psychoanalysis that Hilda was able to fit the pieces together correctly and get over the fears that had built up inside her.

Research studies confirm that adopted girls tend to have more concern over issues of sex and procreation than adopted boys. Perhaps that is only because it is considered unmanly for a boy to appear interested in subjects that arouse one's emotions. But perhaps it is also because women are the ones who get pregnant and bear children. Researcher Susan Farber suggests the feminine identification process is the factor that counts (Farber, 1977: 639–650). She found that adopted girls of school age were especially concerned about problems in bearing a child because of their adoptive mother's problem. Farber suggested that as the girl becomes older, she may choose to identify herself with her birth mother's fertility as a way to cope with her fear that she too may be infertile. Her adoptive mother can help her by accepting her feelings and encouraging that particular aspect of her identification.

Although in our culture, it may be more characteristic of girls to reach out to others when troubled by their feelings, boys need help and reassurance too. They are just as likely to be confused about issues of sexuality and procreation, and suffer just as much from the confusion. Fourteen-year-old Dean Morse is an example.

Adopted at birth, Dean had seemed to understand his parents' explanations about pregnancy, and a pregnant woman's feelings. Although they had given him many opportunities to raise additional questions, he had never shown any interest in issues relating to the carrying of a child. One afternoon, Dean was working in the yard with his father when the older man commented that Dean had seemed to be in low spirits all week. Could he be troubled about something? Dean denied it, merely responding that he was fine, and moving off to trim the hedges with the big clippers. His father let the issue drop.

A few days later, at the dinner table, Dean mentioned his high-school football coach and then referred, in a way his parents recognized as being overly casual, to some things the coach had told the team about his pregnant wife. "Coach said she complained about how hard the baby was kicking her at night," Dean said. Then he asked his mother how an unborn baby could kick a mother. After her careful explanation, the athletic teenager commented that he thought he must have kicked his birth mother a lot. "Probably that's why she got rid of me," he said in an attempted jest that failed to hide the pain of his feelings. Dean's mother quickly expressed her doubt about his conclusion. Dean said no more.

But Dean's parents did not dismiss his remark. They knew he was communicating a problem, and implicitly asking for their help in dealing with it. After talking the matter over privately, they decided to invite the coach and his wife to dinner, to give Dean an opportunity to see for himself how she felt about the baby she was carrying. On the appointed evening, as they sat out on the patio with cool drinks watching the chicken turn golden brown on the barbecue, Dean's mother asked the young woman when her baby was due. On learning that the date was only six weeks away, she observed, "Then I suppose the baby is really kicking now."

"Yes," laughed the mother-to-be. "I'm sure it's going to be a boy, because he's so strong and active. My husband is counting on another football player in the family." She stroked the mound of her stomach with obvious pride, and her husband smiled at her with visible adoration. The talk then turned to the happy preparations the parents were making for their first-born, and Dean's mother felt satisfied that her son had received the message. He had seen the pleasure his coach's wife took in the vitality of her kicking baby, and could make his own clarification of the real meaning of her "complaint."

11 Marriage and Parenthood

As adoptees move into their late adolescent and early adult years, they have an increased need to believe in a personal future that is both predictable and socially acceptable. They are especially concerned about the possibility that a taint of disease or stigma might be attached to their future role as parents. Such a concern, that to others might appear unnecessary or exaggerated, is normal for a person whose birth family background and birth records are concealed. And even when some information has been given, such as that the birth parents' health was good, that they were known to be intelligent and of good background, an adoptee could understandably wonder whether the entire truth was known to anyone. For example, Ann Sorensen, adopted in infancy, married and gave birth in her early twenties to a son who was profoundly deaf, apparently from birth. No reason could be found for his condition. Ann had had a healthy pregnancy and an easy delivery. There was no history of deafness in her husband's family. By default, the onus fell on her own genetic background. As a youngster, she had been given reassuring, although generalized, information about her birth parents, but her obstetrician suggested there must be congenital deafness in her birth family. Ann had no way to determine whether that supposition was true, but she feared she might "taint" another child as she had already "tainted" her son. Therefore, she resolved to have no more children. For many years, she mourned the other children she felt unentitled to bear. Even when she was past child-bearing age, she remained filled with regret over their loss.

The Unknown Genetic Background

The social regulations concerning adoption typically suppress information about the birth family and its genetic heritage. This brings practical problems for the adoptee who is considering future marriage and parenthood. One is the fear of committing actual incest, unwittingly marrying a close blood relative. This is not simply a soap opera fantasy: it does occasionally happen in real life. Perhaps more adoptees, however, are concerned about the kind of plight that Ann Sorensen experienced, the possibility of unknowingly passing on a genetically inherited disease or weakness to their child. And the adoptee must also face other people's fears and biases related to these issues.

Bobbi, adopted at birth, was a vivacious junior majoring in art history at Reed College when she fell in love with a fellow student. At the start of their senior year, he gave her an engagement ring, small but entirely satisfactory to Bobbi's romantic heart, and the couple planned to marry the Christmas after their graduation. But the wedding never took place, as Bobbi explained with tears in her eyes. As the time for the wedding drew near, her fiance seemed to grow cold, withdrawing from her emotionally in an obvious way. When she finally confronted him about his behavior, he told her that he would not want children if he could not know everything about her background. Early in their courtship, Bobbi had confided in him all that she had ever been told about her adoptive situation: She had been born in a state hospital and her birth mother was mentally retarded. Unfortunately, the young woman knew nothing positive about her birth mother—no talent, no winning personality trait—that would help create the image of a whole person rather than the embodiment of a disability. Bobbi concluded that because of the mystery of her birth heritage, her fiance wanted to be released from their engagement but was reluctant to say why. She therefore took the initiative, and he did not protest. Bobbi was bitterly disappointed, and it would take her some time and emotional distance before she could recognize that the broken engagement was due as much to limitations in her fiance's ability to cope with problems as to her own adoptive status.

The past is a powerful determinant of the future, as every student of history knows. Fifteen-year-old Sophie, adopted as an infant, was always very good in that subject at school. On a recent report card, her history teacher had commented, "Sophie goes for the heart of the matter!" Lately, the teenager had been thinking seriously about her birth family background, wondering what the unknown details might be. Her adoptive parents knew little they could pass along, other than that they had been told that her birth mother came to the city as a young girl from a rural environment, somewhere out west, and her birth father was an older married man. Sophie had begun to review these skimpy details and ask herself, "But what do I really know for sure?"

Ever since she was a little girl, one of Sophie's fondest wishes was that she would marry as soon as she finished school and raise a large family. But in her fifteenth year, she had begun worrying about whether she was fully "normal" and whether she would ever be able to become the mother of normal children. She confided her anxiety to her mother, who asked her to define what normal meant; the usually articulate Sophie fumbled and lamely concluded "like everybody else."

Sophie's uneasiness about herself had sprung full-blown recently, when she realized that all her friends had been menstruating "for ages" and she had not yet started. An adolescent's intense concern about getting her period is understandable, for it is a critically important step toward attaining womanhood. For Sophie, the worry was compounded by her unknown genetic background: one who is mystified by the unknown readily attributes the cause of a worry to it. The family doctor had not helped allay her fears, saying of the delay only, "It happens!" Attempted reassurance by her adoptive mother simultaneously disappointed and irritated Sophie. She did not believe that her mother had any rational grounds for her reassurance, since she had no more information about the birth mother than Sophie. And she could not believe that her mother really understood how she felt. She stopped talking to adults about her concerns.

Fortunately, Sophie did not have to remain alone with her feelings for long. She was able to share them with her good friend Sally, who had also been adopted at birth. Unlike Sophie, who tended to be a worrier, Sally had an optimistic personality. Little details that for Sophie had to be just so, like a sweater that was perfectly matched to a skirt, were not important to Sally. "I can be sloppy," she declared definitively. In her younger days, Sally had claimed to her family and friends that she just knew that she had "millions and billions and trillions of OTHER relatives," and she still wished that she could meet some of them, or at least know what they looked like.

The two girls were doing their homework together, books and papers spread out all over Sophie's bed and MTV turned on at full blast. They were collecting materials for a report in their current events class, and it took a while for them to settle down. They talked about whether they liked Madonna better as a blonde or a brunette, and Sally confided she had just thought of something to be really concerned about: how would she and the future father of her imagined baby handle it if the child looked like neither one of them? Or what if she married another adoptee, with no knowledge of his background, like herself?

Though neither Sally nor Sophie could think of a solution to that problem, they did find a solution to Sophie's feeling of being somehow less than normal. While doing their homework, they fortuitously came upon an article published in a 1988 issue of *Newsweek*. According to the report, a noted scientist said that all humankind is descended from a single woman who lived about 200,000 years ago. Said the astonished Sophie, "Why, that means you and I must be cousins, Sally!" Sally agreed. "Yes, and that means that you and your parents are somehow related by blood, and so are my parents and me, and all of us to all of us . . . wow!" Sophie concluded, "So we're all the same, we have the same roots as everybody else." The conversation shifted back to Madonna as the two girls broke out in a fit of giggles over her latest video.

Sally, naturally optimistic and not really aware of feeling different except when Sophie talked to her about it, found the magazine article less noteworthy than did her friend. Sophie cut it out to save, to re-read every now and again when she needed solace. It seemed to contradict that vague feeling of being isolated and different from others that came to her sometimes when she remembered she had been born to a stranger, or when she was worrying about her delayed menstruation. She realized, of course, that the scientific premise of the article had no practical application to her actual life. Nevertheless, being able to reflect on its larger meaning gave her comfort and helped her draw on the inner strength she had developed within the bosom of her adoptive family.

Learning Adult Coping Skills

Parents sometimes fail to recognize—perhaps because they take it so for granted—that they provide the experience from which their children draw emotional strength and the beginnings of wisdom. Sophie's parents, not especially reflective people, probably never congratulated themselves for giving their daughter the kind of emotional stamina that she could draw on, even at those very times in her adolescence when she deliberately and consciously rejected their ideas and judgments as inadequate, as she rejected her mother's assertion that there was nothing wrong with her. Sophie herself was not aware that her parents had taught her a coping skill: how to make herself feel better at those times when she felt down.

The down feeling occurs in everybody's life now and then. The older child's strength to face it originates in the experience of dependency on the mother, which can be taken literally as well as figuratively. Physically, the infant needs to be supported against the mother's body; emotionally the infant depends on her. The mother responds to her child's need in two ways: with her intentions and with her deeds. She wants to comfort her baby; that is the intention. She holds the baby up against her shoulder; that is the deed. Even in infancy, her child senses both her intention and her deed. Their relative importance will change somewhat over the years; for example, the adolescent will care more about a parent's intention and less about the deed. Teenaged Sophie understood in her heart of hearts (though she would not have wanted to admit it) that her adoptive mother's attitude about the menstrual delay came from her maternal inability to think of Sophie as anything but okay.

Occasional feelings of neediness return throughout one's lifetime. It is simply a part of being human. Becoming adept at comforting oneself when feeling needy also lasts, especially when the child is well taught at an early age by loving parents. Identification with their caring intentions begins so early that the young child takes them for granted. In the teen years, when the generation-based communication gap occurs, an adolescent who earlier absorbed enough from the parents can make do with their present seeming or real lack of complete understanding. The teenager often finds what he or she needs by recognizing it outside the family—in a friend, in a book or magazine article, in a teacher, and in the myriad of opportunities that the wider world offers.

Stuart, like Sophie, had been taught good coping skills by his adoptive parents, but in his late adolesence, those skills seemed temporarily to disappear. When he was in college, his solution to the problems that weighed on his mind, primarily his relationship with his girl-friend and his difficulty in choosing a career, was to turn to drugs and alcohol. Heretofore a sensible and reflective young man, Stuart was well aware of the dangers in-volved, and in fact on campus he spoke openly of his resolve to abstain from using either. In secret, however, he broke his resolution. Several times a month, he would join several other students and spend a weekend in the dilapidated apartment of an acquaintance, getting high on a combination of cocaine and expensive cognac.

Stuart unhappily described himself as a "Dr. Jekyll and Mr. Hyde." He meant that he could change from an ordinary state of being to another, extraordinary one. The Mr. Hyde role frightened him even as he compul-sively sought it. The cocaine he shot up caused his heart to beat so fast he thought he might die. The arm he used for the injections felt numb for many hours afterward, and he always feared it might be a sign of an impending stroke. Also, he carelessly used borrowed needles, know-ing that the threat of AIDS was present. Stuart knew his behavior was self-destructive, but he could not quit. He decided to write a good-bye note to his adoptive parents, "just in case," leaving it on his desk at the dorm. The note would tell them that he loved them always, no matter what.

Stuart was intellectually concerned about his irrational behavior, but his desire to change it was weak. The reason for this became clear when he entered therapy about a year after he began his pattern of secret drug abuse. When he sought treatment, through the college mental health program, he said nothing about his drug problem but focused exclusively on his difficulties with his girlfriend and his trouble in making a career choice. Yet perhaps it was his recognition of the underlying problem that really motivated him to get help.

Stuart told his therapist that as long as he could remember, he had had a fantasy about his birth. He believed he had come to earth from a non-human mother. As a young man, the memory of this fantasy consciously amused him, and he remembered that he had always been a fan of Superman, who came to earth from another planet and was raised by a human family. As he remembered more, Stuart said that he was sure he had had to make a "dangerous voyage" to his adoptive family. Yet it had been his fate to survive.

The connection between his present behavior and the fantasy of his birth was inescapable. Stuart had the belief that his birth mother and the child welfare authorities who had been his guardians in his first six months had played Russian roulette with his life. Before they turned him over to his adoptive parents, "I could have died . . . the welfare people were just strangers . . . my birth mother would not have known or cared." Now cocaine had become Stuart's birth mother. He was playing out a game similar to the one he imagined he had been involved in when he was an infant. To survive his drug abuse would mean that he would for a second time survive a dangerous journey: his passage into manhood with its ordinary but often overwhelming problems of love and work.

This interpretation of his past and the way he imagined it to impinge on his present life exhilarated Stuart. He immediately felt released from his driven behavior. The recognition of his problem was not without pain, but his feelings of self-preservation and his anxiety about the dangers of his activities came fully to the fore, helping to motivate the change in his behavior. Since he was not yet at the point of physical addiction, Stuart was able to stop using cocaine. He began work at solving his everyday problems in a more constructive way.

Learning the Full Truth of the Birth Background

Like all children, adoptees in the later years of adolescence and early adulthood are more able to be objective. They are old enough to face the disturbing situation life has burdened them with, and integrate their acceptance into daily life. At this period, an adoptee can and must learn all that the adoptive parents know about the birth family and the circumstances of the adoption. However painful it may be, this is necessary for the adoptee's development and also for the continuing trust in the adoptive parents' truthfulness. The full information should be revealed only when the child is obviously able to understand deviant behavior, although not necessarily ready to accept it. That understanding might come about more readily if the family previously had talked about social problems, perhaps watching television documentaries together, or reading books about such issues as mental illness, alcoholism, child and spouse abuse, homelessness, and the like. Families that are involved in community and religious efforts to give compassionate help to those in need additionally present their adopted children with a home environment in which understanding develops more rapidly.

As parents are preparing the way for the revelation of all known facts about the birth mother, they should take care not to reveal them to others in the immediate or extended family. Otherwise, a slip of the tongue may have a devastating effect on the adoptee.

This is what happened to Donna Gottschalk. She grew up in a large family, long established in the community and active in religious and social affairs. Many in her family, over several generations, were adopted, in continuance of a tradition established at the turn of the century, when the family became outspoken advocates of adoption as a way of sharing the good things the family enjoyed. In comparison with the general population, the Gottschalk family was highly sophisticated in their understanding of adoptive issues. Yet before Donna was fourteen, she was burdened by her older sister with information about her birth mother that she was not ready to handle.

Older sister Millie was nineteen and the biological child of the Gottschalks. The two girls had just watched a TV program that included a segment about an alcoholic mother who lost her children to the authorities after abusing them. The two girls' conversation afterward began in a casual vein, with Millie speculating on what life would be like for a child growing up with abusive parents. Then she went on to wonder what it might have been like for Donna if she had stayed with her alcoholic birth mother and whether her mother would have turned abusive, like the woman they saw on TV.

Recalling that moment years later, Donna said, "My knees turned to jelly!" She had immediately run to her adoptive mother to talk about her discovery. Previously, Donna had been told only that her birth mother could not keep her child because she was a "sick" woman, and Donna had never questioned the statement further. Mrs. Gottschalk confirmed Millie's information, while expressing her own dismay that the older girl had accidentally revealed it. Sensitive to Donna's shattered feelings, she tried to repair the damage by telling Donna that alcoholism is an illness and that she was not in any way responsible for her birth mother's condition. She then reluctantly informed her daughter that her birth mother had been diagnosed as "severely brain damaged" from the alcohol and was committed to an institution.

At the time, Donna, an emotionally well-adjusted teenager, accepted her mother's understanding and comfort. True, her older sister's revelation was ill-timed and misspoken—such information should be revealed only at the proper time and only by the adoptive parents—but it did not cause Donna the severe disruption in her trust of her parents or her belief in herself that it might have brought an adoptee less secure than she was. She tried not to think about, and succeeded, at least, for a while.

Paradoxically, Donna's growing intellectual sophistication as she moved further into her adolescence meant that her worry about the consequences of chemical dependency and the genetic potential for inheritance of alcoholism would increase. The media message that "alcoholism runs in families" struck a responsive chord in Donna, and she experienced occasional upsurges of anxiety based on her increased understanding of the problem.

Donna confided her worries in her best friend, Dell, one afternoon as the two girls stopped for a snack at the mall after school. Her friend's initial response was not encouraging. Dell compared Donna's birth mother to the "crazies" the two girls saw on their occasional Saturday visits to the big city. The next day, Dell's reaction went from bad to worse.

Donna was passionately interested in an older boy, and she decided to take the emotionally risky step of inviting him to participate in a money-raising charity walk sponsored by her church, with a party afterward. He turned her down abruptly. Donna immediately telephoned Dell, sounding as upset as any teenage girl would be in that situation. Donna wanted to rush over to Dell's house to rehash the whole humiliating story with her, but Dell put her off, giving a vague excuse. Then she hung up on Donna and didn't call back to ask how she was doing, or offer to drop by and see her. The next day, when Donna finally saw Dell in the school cafeteria, Dell coolly voiced her opinion that Donna was so upset she might be planning to "cut a wrist, maybe even commit suicide!" Dell said emphatically that she wanted no part of it. Donna felt as shocked as she had when she learned her mother was an alcoholic. She interpreted her friend's reaction to mean, "She thinks *I* am a crazy, otherwise why would I want to cut my wrists?" In one's teen years, the attitude of friends counts for as much or more than that of parents. Dell hurt Donna deeply by withdrawing when Donna badly needed a friend, and then stigmatizing Donna as well.

Donna's way of trying to heal the hurt caused by her friend was to withdraw from sharing her deepest concerns with her peers. Not until she was a freshman in college did she make another close friend, an adoptee like herself, whom she felt she could trust. As it turned out, her new friend was a member of a discussion group for adoptees with concerns similar to Donna's own. To hear others talk, and then eventually take the plunge and talk about herself, with no fear of causing dismay in her listeners, brought Donna a deep sense of security.

Not long after joining the group, Donna came to the decision that she would try to find her birth mother and her birth mother's family. She needed to know more than the vague information she had been given. She felt she had to know what her birth mother's emotional and physical problems were, so she could think rationally about her own future, and especially the potential risks of parenthood. Unlike most adoptees, Donna was successful in her search. She later told the group about her encounter. "My birth mother was living alone in a single-room-occupancy hotel. It was sad, but I didn't have strong feelings one way or the other. She was cordial to me, but the meeting didn't seem to mean anything to her. She acted like she was burned out. Maybe it was the medication she was taking, or the damage due to the years of alcoholism. Through her I met my birth grandmother, though, that was one good thing." Donna subsequently visited her birth grandmother, and met some of her cousins, whom she liked immediately. Family members told Donna that no one understood how her mother got into so much trouble. Donna learned that none of her other blood relatives abused alcohol, and they seemed to lead quiet respectable middle-class lives. Knowing that helped Donna come to terms with her birth heritage, and battle with her fears about the genetic potential she would pass along to her own biological children.

Donna's final task in her struggle to come to terms with the unsavory facts in her background that had hit her like a ton of bricks when she was a teenager was to deal with the attitudes of her adoptive family. She regretted that her parents had themselves been unable to talk about their feelings in regard to her birth background. Donna was the one to show them how.

It was a lengthy process. "First," she explained, "I brought home some literature about birth parents and talked to my parents about what they read. I got the pamphlets through my group. Eventually I took my parents to one of the meetings, and after that, it was easy! It was a matter of showing them that it was really important to me to be able to talk to them about it. I think they knew that instinctively, but they needed to hear from me that I wasn't afraid of the subject. They were afraid that I was afraid."

Information gathered by adoption researchers about the phenomenon of searching for information and reunion with the birth family indicates that considerations related to assuming biological parenthood frequently prompts the search (Sorosky, Baron, and Pannor, 1978). Some adoptees, however, undertake the search for other reasons. Not until she was thirty-five years old was Joyce motivated to join an organization of searchers. The mother of two teenagers, Scott and Patty, Joyce had no interest in searching for her birth family until her daughter began to ask about her background. As Patty put it, "Why do I have to miss out on blood relatives just because you did?" Joyce was surprised to learn that her husband and son also supported Patty's suggestion.

Joyce's start in life was not typical of most adoptees. She had been a foundling, a child who is truly abandoned. While the feeling of being abandoned is probably common to all adopted children at some time during their development, few in reality have suffered that fate. Most come into adoption because the birth mother arranges for it, or at least for the foster care that brings adoption in its wake. But Joyce's story was different. According to contemporary newspaper accounts of the event, an infant five days old, prettily wrapped in a pink blanket with a pink ribbon in her hair, was left by a teenaged girl, presumably her birth mother, with an attendant in a ladies room, in Boston's busy North Station. The girl asked the attendant to hold the baby "for five minutes" while she went to make a phone call—and never returned. The Boston police tried to trace her, without success. The infant was placed in a children's home, and when no one turned up to claim her, she was offered by the State of Massachusetts for adoption.

Joyce was adopted when she was six months old. Her parents handled the original telling very carefully, doing their best to convey a positive attitude toward her background that would help their daughter maintain a good sense of self-esteem. They used hypothetical statements to flesh out the two facts they knew for certain: that her mother was a teenager and that she dressed her baby carefully in a pretty pink outfit. Although her parents had been given the newspaper clippings about the case at the time they adopted Joyce, they did not show them to her when she was a youngster. They did, however, preserve them carefully, and when Joyce was eighteen, they gave her a brown manila envelope filled with yellowed crumbling newspaper accounts of her abandonment.

When Joyce finally learned the facts about herself, she was able to take them with relative calm. She had been prepared, because her parents had carefully explained to her about the enormous social and religious pressures that would have been put on a young unwed mother living in a New England town at the time Joyce was born. After Joyce read the clippings, they told her their assumption that her birth mother must have come to Boston from an outlying town to give birth in the big city's anonymity. Furthermore, they concluded she had intended to take the baby back home on the train, but panicked at the last moment and left the baby behind, under the pretext of making a call. Once she had left the baby, returning to claim her later would have been even harder, because of all the notoriety the case had attracted.

These were comforting ideas for eighteen-year-old Joyce. Even if they could not be confirmed, they were based on rational deduction. The sympathetic and thoughtful attitude of Joyce's parents toward her birth mother's plight—if not toward the impulsive act of giving her baby away in that distressingly casual fashion—helped Joyce retain her good feelings about herself. Later, it provided a model for the point of view that she needed, augmenting her courage when she decided to institute her search.

Joyce began by joining the adoptee activist group in her community. Members helped her with specific advice on how to proceed. They gave her emotional support as she reported hitting one obstacle after another in her attempt to unveil the secret of the beginning of her life. One of the clippings indicated that the police had been able to locate what they assumed were the hospital records of the abandoned infant's birth, but the birth mother gave a false name and address. Joyce hoped she could nevertheless learn something from those records and was disappointed to learn that a fire at the hospital had destroyed them. Then she speculated that her birth mother might have spent some time at a Boston home for unwed mothers known to be patronized by out-of-town teenagers. But she learned that the home no longer existed, and no one had any idea what had become of its files.

After all these disappointments, Joyce felt she had come to a dead end. Yet she had no intention of giving up, even though she had largely depleted her reserves of time and money in the fruitless search. Her sympathetic parents sent her a check to help her continue. She had heard from her adoptees' group that an ad in the Personals column of the newspapers sometimes brought results, and she decided to try it. "I'm so proud of you, Mother," said her daughter Patty. Joyce was brought up short. In the course of her struggle to find information, she had lost sight of what had prompted her to start. "Some day, some day," she said, with all the optimism she could summon. Patty picked up the reference to a story she had loved in childhood and echoed, "Some day, some day, we'll all say, 'How do you do? How good to meet you! We hope you feel the same!'" The family would support Joyce's continuing search.

The Loss of Blood Ties

Few people ordinarily concern themselves about whether or not they feel "real." Those who are conscious of feeling other than real, or to put it another way, feeling unreal—suffer intensely. Feeling unreal is the kind of temporary emotional experience often associated with a major loss, such as the death of someone close or the breakup of a marriage. Sometimes, for no discernible reason, a person who is not going through any major upheaval in relationships is nevertheless affected by the feeling of the unreality of the self. In that case, the problem is usually related to long-standing and hidden emotional difficulties.

Many adoptees who are happy well-adjusted individuals also speak of occasionally feeling not real. Some describe it as being like the deprivation felt by American blacks who mourn the loss of their African heritage. The adoptee, too, has lost a vital ingredient of life, rightfully possessed by all human beings. Life is unthinkable without birth parents and their blood ties to one's self, but adoptees have lost that connection. Worse, their loss of all connection to the birth family is sanctioned by society itself.

Standing in a cluster of graduate students, Aaron chatted with some of his colleagues. They were all studying for a master's degree in social work. The group had just attended a class on the psychological problems of children. They were shaken up by the content of the lecture, which had dealt with diagnosing depression in the young child. Aaron, married to a charming wife and the father of two attractive children, was viewed as a leader by other students. Already experienced as a social worker, he had come back to school to get the formal credentials he lacked for promotion. He had been promised an important executive position once he obtained his graduate degree.

Aaron surprised the rest of the group when he revealed that he had a strong identification with the troubled children who were the subject of the lecture. He explained that he had been adopted in early childhood, by a good loving family and remained very close to his adoptive parents and brother. Although he had spent some time in a children's home before his adoption, he didn't remember the experience and was sure he had not been a depressed child. He was adamant about the point that his problem had started when he was older, much older.

"I have the feeling even now," he confessed. "When I became aware of the complete and total disconnection between me and the people of my own blood, it seemed as if a hole opened up in my heart. You know, a baby born with a hole in the heart is operated on immediately and doesn't know anything about it until old enough to understand what the surgery was all about. The significance does not dawn all at once, but gradually creeps in, more and more disturbing. . . . I too feel much worse now than I did as a teenager, because I understand more now."

At the time of this casual conversation, Aaron did not belong to any organized adoptive search group. Later, he joined the local chapter of a national organization that lobbies to change the state laws controlling access to birth records. Its members also counsel one another in how to get information unobtainable by conventional channels. Like most of those who search for information about their birth heritage, Aaron did not achieve access to his birth papers or learn the name of his birth mother. Even so, being involved with others who thought and felt as he did helped his personal healing process, "at least to the degree that it is possible," Aaron qualified.

Probably all adoptees wonder about their unknown bloodlines, about the geographical localities and birth family names associated with them, about their birth relatives, and most of all about their birth parents. However, most choose not to follow up on their curiosity. Aside from personal feelings of rejection that are difficult to overcome, they put curiosity aside to spare the feelings of their parents. They worry that their adoptive parents will feel rejected by their interest in looking for their birth parents. They are concerned, too, for the feelings of those to whom they owe their beginnings of life, fearing that their birth parents might feel intruded upon, betrayed or angry about their loss of privacy.

Aaron pointed out the universal significance of blood as the basis of relationships. "Blood tells," goes the adage, meaning that blood relationships define a person, and a person identifies with blood ties. Aaron had been reading a work by the eminent British scholar Richard Titmuss (Titmuss, 1971). He read a passage to his fellow students that he especially appreciated.

> For centuries . . . in all cultures and societies, blood has been regarded as a vital, and often magical life-sustaining fluid, marking all important events in life, marriage, birth, initiation and death, and its loss has been associated with disgrace, disgust, impotence, sickness and tragedy. Symbolically and functionally, blood is deeply embedded in religious doctrine; in the psychology of human relationships; and in theories and concepts of kinship, ancestor worship and the family. From time immemorial, it has symbolized qualities of fortitude, vigor, nobility, purity and fertility. Men have been terrified by the thought of blood; they have killed each other for it; they

have believed it could work miracles; and have preferred death rather than receive it from a member of a different ethnic group.

It was to this important truth, the multiple meanings of one's own blood, explained Aaron, that he was expected to be indifferent. "Someday our adoptee organizations are going to change that," he vowed.

12 Communication: The Singular Tie

The shared experience of communication has a special importance for members of an adoptive family, for it is the tie that binds them all together. Unlike the biological family, in which blood inheritance is an important tie, the adoptive family relies solely on shared speech, expression, touch to build a shared history. Communication conveys the parents' attitudes, feelings, and explanations about being adopted to the child, and returns the child's feelings and attitudes back to the parents. The bond that unites in the adoptive family bears strains which other families usually need not face.

The How of Answering a Question

The child who asks a question wants a satisfying answer. Do you remember five-year-old Jeffrey, in chapter 3? He asked his father, "Why are my eyes blue when yours and Mommy's are brown?" His father satisfied him by answering, "In some families, children do look different. There are some reasons for it, but it is too soon for me to explain it to you now. We'll talk about it again when you are eight." That answer satisfied Jeffrey because it conveyed both information and comfort about a situation that puzzled him.

The children depicted in the questions at the end of chapter 1 asked their questions to satisfy several kinds of needs. The questions themselves were reports to their parents on the state of the child's inner world, what was being felt and what was being perceived. At the same time, the children were seeking factual information as well. The question, "Why didn't I come out of your stomach? Why couldn't I have?", for example, is a cry from a child who wants comforting, but the question also seeks information about the nature of adult problems and the adoptive family relationship. Getting that information, in addition to receiving solace, eventually brings more satisfaction to the adoptee than simple comforting alone ever could. It prepares the growing child for grappling with the adult issues that must later be confronted.

The questions a child asks about adoption are sometimes difficult for a parent to answer. For these are issues about which adoptive parents may themselves have strong, and often ambivalent, feelings. Often they feel angry and disapproving about the behavior of the birth parents, at the same time that they are grateful to them for creating the life of the child they cherish. Their own infertility may be an emotional issue that mingles negative feelings about their own incapacity with positive feelings about the child who came to them as a result. They welcome adoption as the way to have a family of their own but may have trouble with the feeling of being different from other families. Parents who have resolved their own problems are usually able to be more relaxed and more spontaneous when they are faced with their child's need to know about origins and identity, or to cope with feelings of bewilderment and hurt.

A Key to the Answers

All the questions at the end of chapter 1 were really asked by adopted children, and their words are given verbatim. The responses are also all genuine remarks suggested by parents to give to their adopted children, when faced in real life with that question or a similar one. In some of the subsequent chapters, expanded versions of these vignettes help explain how the concerns raised in the questions related to other things the child was thinking or worrying about. The stories remind us that these questions, like all others, were not isolated queries but part and parcel of the ceaseless flow of thoughts and feelings that all children experience continually as they wonder about life and the way their world works.

The answers to the questions can be roughly grouped into five styles of communication between adoptive parent and child. The five styles are: Authoritarian, Chosen Baby, Glorifying, Rational, and Reflecting. Look at the key below to see the style of each answer.

1. Mrs. Gardner is undressing three-year-old Jimmy, preparing him for bed. Obviously not yet ready to go to sleep, the boy has been interrupting her constantly. From out of the blue he asks, "Did my 'other' mother give me a toy when I was very little? If she did, I want it!"

_____ **A.** I am sure your "other mother" gave you a toy. GLORIFYING

_____ **B.** It's time for a good little boy to stop asking questions and go to bed. AUTHORITARIAN

_____ **C.** You have lovely toys now, so it shouldn't matter. CHOSEN BABY

_____ **D.** Of course you are curious about things you don't remember. REFLECTING

_____ **E.** I don't know, I would have to find out for you. I'll call your social worker in the morning and ask. RATIONAL

2. Ten-year-old Skye looks away from the family TV and fidgets for awhile. Then she asks, "Even if I knew my natural mother's name and where she lives, I don't want to see her. She probably has a family now. What would she want to see me for?"

_____ **A.** Of course, you never have to see her. But you might change your mind when you are older. RATIONAL

_____ **B.** Yes, your natural mother probably has a family now, and is sure and confident that you are loved and happy. GLORIFYING

_____ **C.** You're right, children don't need to worry about make-believe. You've been with us so long, I am your real parent. AUTHORITARIAN

_____ **D.** Okay, if you don't want to see her, you don't have to. Just think about the family and the love you have now. CHOSEN BABY

___ **E.** You are wondering about what your natural mother is doing now. It's okay to think about her. REFLECTING

3. Mark is six years old. He is sitting at the dinner table with a dreamy look on his face. While everyone else eats, he plays with his fork. Then he starts to talk about what his "other" mother was like. He asks, "What was *her* mommy and daddy like—I'm thinking about all of them."

___ **A.** I don't know. Anyway, you are with us now, and we think you are special. CHOSEN BABY

___ **B.** You'd like to know all about your other family and what their lives were like when they were children like you. REFLECTING

___ **C.** I really can't answer your questions. Maybe when you are older, we can find out the answers together. RATIONAL

___ **D.** Your "other" mother was a terrific person, and your biological grandparents were probably a lot like your adoptive grandparents. GLORIFYING

___ **E.** I don't know about them. But a child doesn't need more than one family, and you know all about us and our parents. AUTHORITARIAN

4. Eight-year-old Kate, dressed for school, is sitting at the kitchen counter waiting for her mother to finish packing her lunchbox. She talks about being at a friend's house the previous afternoon, and how her friend looks just like her older sister. Kate asks, "Why can't I look like somebody besides just me, too?"

_____ **A.** You'd like it if we looked like a family. But we are a family anyway. REFLECTING

_____ **B.** You probably look like your biological family, the way your friend looks like hers. RATIONAL

_____ **C.** You are much loved, and that is more than lots of biological children could say for themselves. CHOSEN BABY

_____ **D.** It isn't important for a child to resemble anybody in the family physically. Lots of children don't. AUTHORITARIAN

_____ **E.** You are a very special person. You just look good by yourself. GLORIFYING

5. Linda is helping her mother take the dishes out of the dishwasher and put them away. The eight-year-old suddenly asks, "Why didn't I come out of your stomach? Why couldn't I have?"

_____ **A.** It would have been nice, but you came to me in a special kind of way. RATIONAL

_____ **B.** If you had come out of me, then you wouldn't be gorgeous, like your natural mother. GLORIFYING

_____ **C.** Because that's the way God wanted it. AUTHORITARIAN

_____ **D.** It doesn't matter where you come from but how much you are wanted, and we love you very much. CHOSEN BABY

_____ **E.** You wonder if maybe you are really my natural child after all, and feel you'd like to know all about your birth. REFLECTING

6. Eight-year-old David looks up from the homework he is doing, then asks his adoptive mother a question. "Why does it still hurt that my natural mother had me and then gave me up?"

_____ **A.** I don't know . . . she gave you up because she wanted you to have a good home, like ours. GLORIFYING

_____ **B.** It's not necessary for children to think about these things, and then they don't get hurt. AUTHORITARIAN

_____ **C.** I don't really know, but I have you now, and I'm sure glad, because I love you very much. CHOSEN BABY

_____ **D.** You're feeling sorry right now that you don't know her, or see her. REFLECTING

_____ **E.** It might always hurt. It is a very tough experience to go through. RATIONAL

7. Andrea Johnson and her nine-year-old Margie look very different from one another. On a week-long vacation in a rented beach house, they go into a grocery store to buy food for dinner. Margie covers her face with the hood of her jacket; when her mother tells her not to do that, the girl answers defiantly, "I want to." She explains that people are staring at her because she looks so different from her mother. She adds that she thinks the other shoppers know she is not "from" her mother. "Why can't I cover my face?" she asks.

_____ **A.** Children can't read people's minds. What these people in the grocery store think doesn't matter anyhow. AUTHORITARIAN

_____ **B.** You have nothing to be ashamed of, because you are loved as much as anyone's children can be loved. CHOSEN BABY

_____ **C.** You are wondering what people think about us being together. REFLECTING

_____ **D.** People can look different, like flowers are different. RATIONAL

_____ **E.** Don't cover yourself up . . . maybe the other people here would like to get to know you. GLORIFYING

8. Ten-year-old Matthew comes home from school and complains that the other children are teasing him because he is adopted. "How can I get them to stop?" he asks.

_____ **A.** Life is like that. All children get teased sometimes. I'll talk to their parents, or you can handle it on your own. AUTHORITARIAN

_____ **B.** Tell them how special you are because you were chosen. They weren't chosen, they were just born. CHOSEN BABY

_____ **C.** You're mad at the other kids for teasing you and frustrated because they don't stop. Maybe you are having trouble explaining to them what being adopted means. REFLECTING

_____ **D.** If you don't appear to get upset at the teasing, they will get tired of it, I think. RATIONAL

_____ **E.** Try not to let it bother you, because people only tease someone they like. GLORIFYING

9. Eleven-year-old Ronny is supposed to be cleaning his room, but he is dawdling. When his father reminds him he needs to finish his task, Ronny says, "I used to be very embarrassed to be adopted." Then he asks, "Do you know why?"

____ A. Be proud, Ronny. Children are generally proud to be adopted. GLORIFYING

____ B. It doesn't really matter, a lot of children are adopted. AUTHORITARIAN

____ C. Just think, we picked you out because we wanted you. CHOSEN BABY

____ D. Perhaps you still feel that way and don't like that feeling. REFLECTING

____ E. When you aren't sure it is okay to be a certain way, you can be embarrassed. RATIONAL.

10. Twelve-year-old Vincent is putting a dimmer switch on the light fixture over the dining table. He turns to his adoptive parents and asks, "How come I am so handy, when you both are not?"

____ A. It's God's will that some children can do things and some cannot. It has nothing to do with how we are. AUTHORITARIAN

____ B. We are the lucky ones to have you around. Just imagine what it would be like here if you weren't around to help us out. CHOSEN BABY

____ C. You have a gift of fixing things, and it is important to you. REFLECTING

____ D. You inherited some talents from your natural parents and perhaps you just developed your handiness on your own. RATIONAL

_____ E. You're just really a terrific kid—what can I say?
    GLORIFYING

Interestingly, most of the answers given by the parents of the children who actually asked the questions in chapter 1 fell into the same category, the Rational type of answer. The Rational style is factual, unequivocally truthful, and utilizes high-level modes of reasoning. Yet even a three-year-old can grasp a hypothetical statement like the one given by Jimmy's mother: "Perhaps she gave you a toy. I don't know. I'll have to find out for you."

Of course, the answer that satisfies a three-year-old's capacity for reason will not do for a teenager. As a child develops, a satisfying answer changes both in regard to content and to the means of reassurance. Using babyhood words might comfort Jimmy but would drive an adolescent into huffy withdrawal. Still, the *how* of the response, the underlying strategy, remains the same at all ages, even for adults.

The Rational style is grounded in the adoptee's external reality: other people in the environment and their attitudes; objects and processes; past history and future expectations; the questioner's own attributes and behavior as seen by others. Because it is not ambiguous and does not present false information, it stimulates a youngster to think clearly about the ambiguities of life. The Rational style also validates the child's questioning attitude. The parent offers the child some decision-making opportunities, and the "we-ness" of the family can be emphasized. Notice the Rational style of response to Mark's question in Question #3. In regard to Mark's interest in knowing about his mysterious birth mother, his adoptive father said that although he could not answer the question now, perhaps when Mark was older they could look for answers together.

The Rational style highlights the concept of options that the parent presents to the child. In Question #7, Margie's situation, the child learns that she could accept the reality that she differs in appearance from her mother because nature itself approves of differences. Nature makes flowers beautiful and different from one another. Learning to exercise judgment through the consideration of alternatives is important in the development of all children because it leads to independence of thought and action, and eventually to the ability to take care of oneself and others in adult life. It may be especially important to an adoptee, who faces a powerful societal demand that the curious child remain passive about important personal information. And the language that shares with the child the parent's power to make decisions and authority of knowledge enhances the child's process of identification with the parent. That, in turn, gives him or her the sense of truly belonging, a sense that is the cornerstone of the adoptive family structure.

The chief liability of the Rational style can be its seeming coldness and lack of emotional support. Dealing only with the factual content of the question may fail to provide the comfort youngsters are implicitly seeking. Thus it may be preferable to pair the Rational style with another, more comforting style of dialogue. A good choice would be the Reflecting style.

In the Reflecting style, the parent gives an answer that mirrors the feelings contained within the child's question. This identifies the often inchoate feelings of the child, validates them, and asserts that they are worthy of respect. And that explicit information encourages a child in the very act of asking a question. The Reflecting style shares with the Rational style its truthfulness and avoidance of ambiguity; it may also employ logic to make its point. Look at the way the Reflecting style works in Question #1. The wording tells Jimmy that it is okay to be curious about his birth mother. Thus it reassures the boy that *he* is okay. It will encourage Jimmy to ask more questions about the issues that concern him, and to share his feelings with his parents.

The Reflecting style communicates a parent's comfort to a child. But, used alone, it may not give the child enough information. Many parents interviewed about the questions tended not to like the Reflecting style. Some called it "too therapeutic"—and it is true that child therapists typically use this approach. A Columbia professor commented that a child might find the Reflecting style emotionally intrusive; it could seem more like prying than reflecting the child's own feelings. One irate father who reviewed the questions denounced the reflecting style as "unreal" and "PET-oriented" (a reference to Parent Effectiveness Training, a parenting program developed by Dr. Thomas Gordon.)

Another style that might pair with the Rational style to add comfort to its information is the Chosen Baby style. A parent using the Chosen Baby style emphasizes the notion that the adopted child is specially loved because he or she has been specially chosen by the parents. The intention is to support the child's sense of self-esteem by a reminder of the immense and unconditional love offered by the adoptive family. An incident reported by an adoptive mother illustrates how useful the Chosen Baby style can be to an older child in a situation that creates strong emotions. Alexandra, adopted in her infancy, was about to celebrate her sixteenth birthday. She was initially pensive, then distraught, as she began to wonder whether the significance of the day would have any meaning to her birth mother. Alexandra had been born to a severely disturbed patient in a state hospital for the chronically ill, and her mother had relinquished her at birth. Now the girl was bitterly hurt by her logical assumption that her landmark sixteenth birthday would mean nothing to her birth mother.

Luckily, Alexandra's adoptive mother recognized that her daughter's distress had nothing to do with her present life in her adoptive family, but only indicated her sorrow over the long-ago event of being given away. Grasping for words, she did her best to console her daughter for that hurt. "I don't know anything about your birth mother's feelings, but I have you and I love you and I am very glad that you are with me. You make me happy that you are here." Thus she offered her own love as a substitute for the birth mother's and as a reparation for the early wound of being given away. In this case, the use of the Chosen Baby style was sound. However, in a situation like Jimmy's (Question #1) the child is not asking for consolation but simply seeking information. In that case, the Chosen Baby style might seem like a manipulation of his emotions, and also perhaps convey the subtle message that asking such questions is upsetting to the family. Another danger inherent in the Chosen Baby style is that it overemphasizes the child's dependence on the adoptive parents' love as the answer to a problem and diminishes the importance of the child's ability to think things over autonomously.

On some occasions, parents might choose to offer comfort through the use of the Glorifying style. The Glorifying style idealizes the adoptee, the birth parents, and the birth background. The Glorifying style makes outright statements or strong implications that the birth parent and birth heritage are good—great—SUPER-GREAT! The parent who uses this style usually perceives the child's question as an appeal for self-esteem. Other important aspects of the question, such as the child's curiosity and interest in grasping the ambiguities of adoptive life may be overlooked. Some of the statements made by a parent using the Glorifying style may well be true, but the adoptive parent does not really know that for a fact, and the answers are not presented as hypotheses but as truths. Thus, the Glorifying style often disappoints the child's growing grasp of reality. At the same time, it fails to offer the adoptee the chance to learn how to use the tools of logical reasoning to deal with problems. It may eventually create confusion in the child's view of reality, or distrust of the adoptive parents. Sometimes, as in Margie's case (Question #7) when the Glorifying style makes light of the child's anxiety (displayed by her attempt to cover her face) it is not supportive of the child's real feelings.

The Glorifying style is best used, judiciously, with the younger child who needs to view everything about the birth parents and birth heritage as positive. For a child like Jimmy, giving a Glorifying response rather than a Rational one might help support his immature sense of himself as good. But to talk the same way to a teenager could result in the despairing conclusion that the adoptive parents themselves cannot handle the ambiguity with which the adoptee must forever live.

A hundred years ago, the Authoritarian style was considered the proper way to speak to a child. Embodied by the familiar adage "children should be seen and not heard," the Authoritarian style views parent/child communication as a one way street: the parent talks and the child listens. Today, this style is much less popular, with parents and child development specialists alike. Yet parents who feel comfortable with the Authoritarian style, which is designed not so much to teach as to silence the child, can use it effectively. An example can be seen in the story of Ben in chapter 3. His mother was unable to come up with a good answer to Ben's question about why it wasn't men who gave birth to baby boys, but his grandmother, using the Authoritarian style, satisfied Ben by saying, "Because God wanted it that way." It was the right answer from the right person, but Ben's mother would not have been comfortable giving it.

Many parents, especially younger ones, may feel uneasy about answering questions in the Authoritarian style. They recognize that it may force a child to suppress or deny feelings, rather than helping resolve them. Yet look at the Authoritarian answer to Question #8, where a boy asks how to get the other children to stop teasing him: "Life is like that. All children get teased sometimes. I'll talk to their parents or you can handle it on your own." This answer doesn't leave the child room to discuss anything further, except whether or not to let the parent take the situation out of the child's hands. Yet it is a reply that firmly suggests that the adoptee is no different from other children, and therefore may convey both comfort and significant information.

Using Other People's Words

Many adoptive parents fear their own skills of communication are inadequate for the task of informing and comforting their children. A powerful, yet unobtrusive, tool for communication can be found in literature. Many works, from the great classics to the comic strips, deal with themes that underlie adoptive life. The fairy tale "Thumbelina," for example, tells of how a tiny girl who was born in a tulip and adopted by a peasant woman finally finds her identity through her own efforts. Rudyard Kipling's *Jungle Book* tells the story of Mowgli, the infant adopted by Father and Mother Wolf. Henry Fielding's classic novel *Tom Jones* has a hero who is a foundling and must overcome the stigma of his illegitimacy. The Biblical story of Moses tells of a mother's willingness to relinquish her child in the hope of saving his life. Oscar Wilde's play *The Importance of Being Ernest* deals in a humorous way with the plight of a foundling who claims his only known relative is the leather bag in which he was left at a train station.

Literary works that deal with themes of adoptive life in the words of a writer who has spent much time and effort in learning to say things effectively can be a good tool for family communication. In a book, the child can confront such subjects as the mystery of an adoptee's origins, the motives of birth parents in giving up their children, or the fantasies of being from another race (or another planet) from a safe emotional distance. The timing is under the child's own control; a book can be closed when it strikes too close to the deepest emotions, and reopened when the child is ready to continue the confrontation. The reading child can consider powerful adoptive themes without being overwhelmed by them. Parents can make the reading a family affair, or they can allow the child to digest the book in private. They can wait until the child asks questions about what has been read, or they can initiate family discussions about the issues. With parental guidance and support, literary works can be one of the best forms of family communication.

Silence as Communication

Silence should not be confused with the absence of communication. Saying *nothing* can convey a powerful message. It can communicate anger, or indifference, or disapproval, or complete withdrawal. As we saw in chapter 9, when silence is used as a form of discipline, it can arouse great anxiety in an adopted child, who may fear the silence is a prelude to another act of abandonment. Like other aspects of adoptive life, however, silence can have more than one meaning. The silence of loving adoptive parents can sometimes be a blessing, on those occasions when the child feels so vulnerable in regard to an adoptive issue that he or she cannot bear to deal with it in words. A tender gesture, or a loving look, may at such times be the best possible form of communication: a way to say, "I understand that this is painful for you, and I respect your feelings."

Even so, for a child to be able to put needs into words, and to feel free to ask questions and voice concerns, is always a worthy goal in a parent-child relationship. Particularly as a youngster nears the end of adolescence, parents should try to reopen the pathways of family conversation about adoption, even though they may have been closed by the teenager's need for increased privacy.

Connie and Stan remembered what their adopted son Jim had been like in high school. Although he had been an articulate youngster, after he reached his teens, he no longer wanted to talk to his parents. When his grades slipped, and the issue of being black in a white family became troublesome to him, he avoided discussing how he felt about either issue. His parents would have liked to share his feelings, but he rebuffed their attempts to raise the subject. Their strategy for unobtrusively letting their son know they cared was an interesting one. At times when the family was together, Connie and Stan would sometimes start reminiscing about their own adolescence: talking about their own teenaged problems (some of which were actually quite similar to Jim's) and the ways they tried to solve them. Occasionally, one of them would turn to Jim and say, "That was what it was like for me. I guess you are experiencing something similar . . . do you think things have changed?" Jim would listen silently, without responding to their questions.

When Jim left high school, he got a job at the local YMCA and continued to live at home. Gradually, he began to initiate the custom of knocking on his parents' bedroom door in the evenings after he got home from work, wanting to talk to them about anything and everything: current events, local gossip, family affairs, and the boys in the classes he led.

Although Jim was more talkative, that did not mean that he was ready to share his deepest concerns with his parents. Connie and Stan had no illusions on that score, nor did they believe that if they knew his problems they would be able to solve them. They did, however, comfort themselves with the thought that family communication is an ongoing process. There would be many future opportunities to talk, and to talk about a wider range of topics in greater depth. There would always be a chance to "say things better."

Although Connie and Stan did not consider themselves highly skilled communicators, they had succeeded in getting their message of love and concern across to their son. In one of their evening chats, they asked Jim what had happened to make him so much more talkative. He answered simply: "I knew I could always talk to you before, but that is not what I wanted. Now it is." He concluded, "Even when I didn't answer you, I heard what you said."

Bibliography

Chapter One

Feigelman, W., and Silverman, A., *Chosen Children*. New York: Praeger Publishers, 1983.

Lawder, E.A., Lower, K.D., Andrews, R.G., Sherman, E.A., and Hill, J.G., "A Follow-up Study of Adoptions: Post-placement Functioning of Adoption Families." New York: Child Welfare League of America, Inc., 1969.

Chapter Two

Brodzinski, D.M., Singer, L.M., and Braff, A.M., "Children's Understanding of Adoption," *Child Development*, Volume 55, pp. 869–878, 1984.

Peller, L., "About 'Telling the Child' About his Adoption." *Bulletin of the Philadelphia Association for Psychoanalysis*, Volume 11, pp. 145–154, 1961.

Simon, N., *All Kinds of Familes*. Niles, IL: Albert Whitman & Co., 1976.

Wieder, H., "On Being Told of Adoption," *The Psychoanalytic Quarterly*, Volume 46, pp. 1–22, 1977.

Winnicott, D.W., *The Maturational Processes and the Facilitating Environment*. New York: International Universities Press, 1974.

Chapter Three

Fassler, J., *Helping Children Cope*. New York: The Free Press, 1978.

Kaplan, L.J., *Oneness and Separateness: From Infant to Individual*. New York: Simon & Schuster, 1978.

Koch, J., *Our Baby*, An Adoption Story. Ft. Wayne, IN: Perspectives Press, 1985.

Chapter Four

Beres, D., "Perception, Imagination and Reality," *The International Journal of Psychoanalysis*, Volume 41, pp. 327–334, 1960.

Bettelheim, B., *The Uses of Enchantment*. New York: Alfred A. Knopf, 1976.

Jewett, C., *Helping Children Cope with Separation and Loss*. Harvard, MA: Harvard Common Press, 1982.

Kaplan, L.J., *op. cit.*

Winnicott, D.W., *op. cit.*

Chapter Five

Anthony, E.J., "Risk, Vulnerability and Resilience: An Overview," in Anthony, E.J., and Cohler, B.J. (eds.), *The Invulnerable Child*. New York: The Guilford Press, 1987.

Malina, L.R., *Raising Adopted Children*. New York: Harper & Row, 1986.

Chapter Six

Bernstein, R., "Unmarried parents and their families," *Child Welfare*, Volume 45, pp. 185–195, 1966.

Cotton, N.S., "The Development of Self-Esteem and Self-Esteem Regulation," in Mack, J.E., and Ablon, S.L. (eds.), *The Development and Sustaining of Self-Esteem in Childhood*. New York: International Universities Press, 1983.

Herzog, E., "Some Notes About Unmarried Fathers," *Child Welfare*, Volume 45, pp. 194–197, 1966.

Mack, J.E., "Self-Esteem and Its Development: An Overview," in Mack and Ablon, *op. cit.*

Nerlove, E., *Who Is David?* New York: Child Welfare League of America, Inc., 1985.

Pope, H., "Unwed Mothers and Their Sex Partners," *Journal of Marriage and the Family*, Volume 29, pp. 555–567, 1967.

Chapter Seven

Feigelman and Silverman, *op. cit.*

Goleman, D., "In Memory, People Recreate Their Lives to Suit Their Images of the Past," *The New York Times*, Section C, p. 1, June 23, 1987.

Kadushin, A., *Adopting Older Children*. New York: Columbia University Press, 1970.

Ladner, J., *Mixed Families*. Garden City, NY: Anchor Press/ Doubleday, 1977.

McRoy, R., Zurcher, L., Lauderdale, M., and Anderson, R., "Self-Esteem and Racial Identity in Transracial and Inracial Adoptees," *Social Work*, November, 1982.

Stern, D., *The Interpersonal World of the Infant*. New York: Basic Books, 1985.

Chapter Eight

Kaplan, L.J., *Adolescence: The Farewell to Childhood*. New York: Simon & Schuster, 1984.

Klein, M., *Envy and Gratitude and Other Works, 1946–1963*. New York: Delacorte Press, 1975.

Lawder, E.A., et al., *op. cit.*

McWhinnie, A., *Adopted Children, How They Grow Up*. London: Routledge and Kegan Paul, 1967.

Winnicott, D.W., *op. cit.*

Chapter Nine

Jaffe, B., and Fanshel, D., *How They Fared in Adoption*. New York: Columbia University Press, 1970.

Kohn, M.L., "Social Class and Parent-Child Relationships," *American Journal of Sociology*, Volume 68, pp. 471–480, 1963.

Peller, L., "Further Comments About Adoption," *Bulletin of the Philadelphia Association for Psychoanalysis*, Volume 13, pp. 1–14, 1962.

Smith, J., and Miroff, F., *You're Our Child*. Washington: University Press of America, 1981.

Winnicott, D.W., *op. cit.*

Chapter Ten

Benet, M.K., *The Politics of Adoption*. New York: The Free Press, 1976.

Bunin, C., and Bunin, S., *Is That Your Sister?* New York: Pantheon Books, 1976.

Cadoret, R.D., et al., "Development of Alcoholism in Adoptees Raised Apart From Alcoholic Biologic Relatives," *Archives of General Psychiatry,* Volume 37, Number 5, pp. 561–562, 1980.

Farber, S., "Sex Differences in the Expression of Adoption Ideas: Observations of Adoptees From Birth Through Latency," *American Journal of Orthopsychiatry,* Volume 47, Number 4, pp. 639–650, 1977.

Kirk, D., *Shared Fate.* New York: Free Press, 1964.

Leitch, D., *Family Secrets.* New York: Delacorte Press, 1984.

Skeels, H.M., "Some Iowa Studies of the Mental Growth of Children in Relation to Differentials of the Environment: A Summary," *Intelligence: Its Nature and Nurture,* 39th Yearbook of the National Society for the Study of Education, Volume 2, pp. 281–308, 1940.

Tizard, B. and Rees, J., "A Comparison of the Effects of Adoption, Restoration to the Natural Mother and Continued Institutionalization on the Cognitive Development of Four-Year-Old Children," *Child Development,* Volume 45, pp. 92–99, 1974.

Chapter Eleven

Sorosky, S., Baron, A., and Pannor, R., *Adoption Triangle.* Garden City, NY: Anchor Press/Doubleday, 1978.

Titmuss, R.M., *The Gift Relationship.* New York: Pantheon Books, 1971.

Chapter Twelve

Komar, M., "Adoptees' Questions About Themselves: The Influence of Social Class on the Adopter's Answer," Doctoral dissertation, Adelphi University School of Social Work. Ann Arbor, MI: University Microfilms International, 1983.

Robinson, W.P., and Rackstraw, S.J., *A Question of Answers,* Volumes 1 & 2. London: Routledge and Kegan Paul, 1972.

Index